This book is to be returned on or before
the last date stamped below.

STUDY UNITS

THE MAKING OF THE UNITED KINGDOM

HEINEMANN
EDUCATIONAL

Joe Scott

Heinemann Library,
an imprint of Heinemann Publishers (Oxford) Ltd,
Halley Court, Jordan Hill, Oxford OX2 8EJ

OXFORD LONDON EDINBURGH MADRID
ATHENS BOLOGNA PARIS MELBOURNE
SYDNEY AUCKLAND SINGAPORE TOKYO
IBADAN NAIROBI HARARE GABORONE
PORTSMOUTH NH (USA)

First published 1993

97 96 95 94 93

10 9 8 7 6 5 4 3 2 1

**British Library Cataloguing in Publication Data is
available from the British Library on request.**

ISBN 0–431–07346–5

Designed by Ron Kamen, Green Door Design Ltd,
Basingstoke

Illustrated by Phill Burrows Jeff Edwards
and Adam Hook

Printed in China

The front cover is from 'Leviathan' by Thomas
Hobbes, 1651.

Acknowledgements

The authors and publishers would like to thank the following
for permission to reproduce photographs:

Achievements Ltd: 5.3A
Bridgeman Art Library: 2.4A, 2.5A, 4.2A, 4.4G, p.59
British Library: 4.2B, 4.4A, 4.4H
J. Allan Cash Ltd: 3.4C, 4.6B, 5.6B
Professor Rex Cathcart: 5.1A
Viscount De L'Isle (private collection): 2.3A
Edifice/Gillian Darley: 3.4D
Mary Evans Picture Library: 4.1B
Fotomas Index: 1.3A, 3.2D, 3.3H, 4.2G, 4.5H, 5.6A
Hulton Picture Company: 1.3D, 4.1C, 4.2C
Ironbridge Gorge Museum: p.59
Mansell Collection: Cover, 1.2A, 2.2B, 3.1C, 3.3A, 3.4A,
4.1A, 4.5B, 5.5C
Museum of London: 4.5A, 4.5G
National Galleries of Scotland: 2.4B
Ann Ronan Picture Library: 4.6A, p.58
Earl of Rosebery: 4.3A

Royal Collection, St. James's Palace © Her Majesty the
Queen: 2.2A, 4.2D, 4.2F, 5.2A
Royal Collection, Windsor Castle © Her Majesty the Queen:
1.2E
Shakespeare Birthplace Trust: 3.3E
Joan Shuter: p.59
Weidenfeld & Nicolson Archives: 1.2D
Woodmansterne: 3.3C, 3.4B
Yale Center for British Art, Paul Mellon Collection: 5.5A

Every effort has been made to contact copyright holders of
material reproduced in this book. Any omissions will be
rectified in subsequent printings if notice is given to the
publisher.

Details of written sources

In some sources the wording or sentence structure has been
simplified to ensure that the source is accessible.

Thomas Beard, 'The Theatre of God's Judgement', 1597. In:
D. Underdown, *Revel Riot and Rebellion*, OUP, 1987: 1.2B
'The Book of Common Prayer', 1559. In: *History Today*,
March, 1984: 1.2C
Hugh Brogan, *Pelican History of the USA*, Pelican, 1986: 5.3C
Daniel Defoe, *Journey Through the Whole of Great Britain, 1724*
(Ed. Pat Rogers), Penguin, 1971: 5.5D
Celia Fiennes, *The Journeys of Celia Fiennes* (Ed. C. Morris),
London, 1947: 5.5B
C. H. Firth, *Clarke Papers*, Camden Society, 1891: 4.4D, 4.4F
S. R. Gardiner, *Constitutional Documents of the Puritan
Revolution*, OUP, 1906: 4.4C
J. Gilingham, 'The Origins of English Imperialism'. In:
History Today, February, 1987: 3.3G
Glossop Parish Overseer's Accounts, 1686, Derbyshire Records
Office: 3.2C
William Harrison, 'Description of England', 1587. In:
J. Dover Wilson, *Life in Shakespeare's England*, Penguin, 1944:
3.1A, 3.1B, 3.1E
Bishop Jewel, 'Zurich Letters', 1559. In: Thomas, 1973: 1.3B
R. McCrum, *The Story of English*, BBC Books, 1986: 3.3F
Sir Thomas More, 'Utopia', 1516. In: N. L. Frazer, *English
History Illustrated from Original Sources, 1485–1603*, Black,
1908: 3.2A
J. E. Neale, *Queen Elizabeth I*, Penguin, 1960: 2.2B, 2.3B, 2.4C
Samuel Pepys, *Diary*, (Eds. R. Latham, W. Mathews Bell),
1970: 4.5C, 4.5D, 4.5E, 4.5F
G. W. Prothero, *Select Statutes and Constitutional Documents,
1559–1625*, OUP, 1913: 2.3C, 3.2B, 4.2E
Paul Shuter, John Child, *Skills in History 2*, Heinemann
Educational, 1989: 4.4B, 4.4E
John Stow, 'Annals', 1605. In: Joe Scott, *Energy Through Time*,
OUP, 1986: 3.1D
Keith Thomas, *Religion and the Decline of Witchcraft*, Penguin,
1973: 1.3C
F. J. Weaver, *English History Illustrated from Original Sources,
1603–1660*, Black, 1908: 5.3B
William Whately, 'The Bridal Bush', London, 1617. In: L.
Stone, *The Family, Sex and Marriage in England 1500–1800*,
Penguin, 1979: 1.2F

CONTENTS

1.1 Disunited Kingdoms

In the years 1500–1750 Britain became much **richer**, more **powerful** and more **united** than before. In 1500, as you can see from the map, many things kept Britain disunited. For instance, Scotland was a separate country with its own king. It took much longer to send a message to the Scottish border than it now takes to travel to Australia.

But things were changing, and some of these changes were working to pull the British Isles more closely together. For instance, the **design of ships** was greatly improved at this time, so it was easier to sail to any part of Britain to trade or to fight. Also, **guns and gunpowder** were coming into use. This meant that the castles of the great lords were no longer safe from attack. Only the **monarch** (king or queen) could really afford an up-to-date army with guns and the skilled soldiers needed to use them.

King Henry VII of England already had the titles 'Prince of Wales' and 'Lord of Ireland'. He and his nobles held castles in all these countries. Henry was partly Welsh, and this probably made Welsh people more loyal to him.

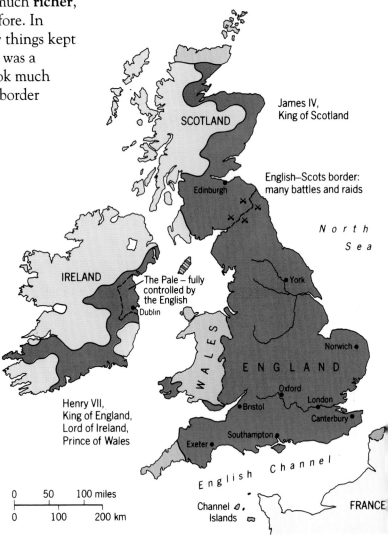

People speak English (but in many different dialects)

People speak Gaelic

People speak Welsh

People speak Cornish

People speak Norse

People speak French but are ruled by English king

• Towns with over 5,000 people

✕ Battles

Henry VII

Henry VII (1457–1509) lived in exile in France after 1471, due to fighting between the families of York and Lancaster. Henry was Lancastrian. In 1485, he beat the Yorkist king at the battle of Bosworth. To help bring peace he married Elizabeth of York.

1.2 Lords and Masters

The monarch and the people.

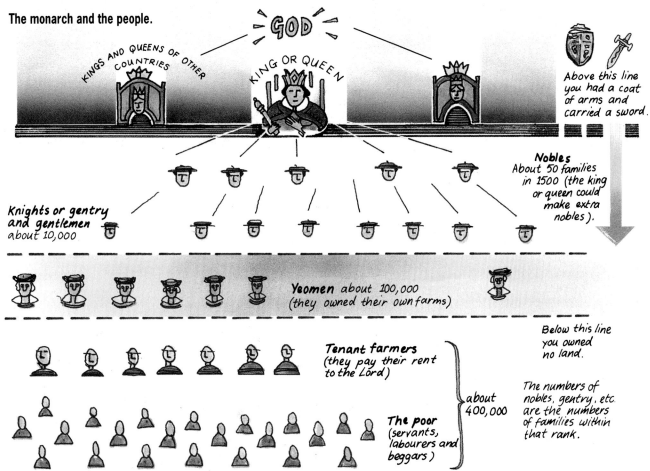

GOD

KINGS AND QUEENS OF OTHER COUNTRIES

KING OR QUEEN

Above this line you had a coat of arms and carried a sword.

Nobles
About 50 families in 1500 (the king or queen could make extra nobles).

Knights or gentry and gentlemen
about 10,000

Yeomen about 100,000
(they owned their own farms)

Below this line you owned no land.

Tenant farmers
(they pay their rent to the Lord)

The poor
(servants, labourers and beggars)

about 400,000

The numbers of nobles, gentry, etc. are the numbers of families within that rank.

As you can see from the diagram, everybody in England in 1500 had someone above them. Above the king or queen was God. If you were a tenant farmer, you were supposed to love, honour and respect your **lord**, the person above you. You showed this by taking your hat off, bowing or even kneeling down when you saw him. If you were a lord or master, you were expected to be kind, generous and helpful to the people of lower rank under your care. Wives and children, even grown-up children, were supposed to obey the 'head of the family'. People thought it very important for sons and daughters to marry into a family of the same rank or higher.

This system was the only one people knew of, and they accepted it just as they accepted the air they breathed. There were always people who broke the rules, but most people knew their position and expected other people to know theirs.

In 1500 there were probably about 2¼ million (2,250,000) people in England. From the monarch down to the poor, everyone knew the level or **rank** to which they belonged. A wife had the same rank as her husband, children the same rank as their father.

Rules of rank

- Only people of lower ranks could be whipped or branded.
- Only gentlemen could carry swords.
- Only gentlewomen could wear silk.

Nine out of ten English people in 1500 lived in little country villages of 500 people or less. The **lord of the manor** was the only gentleman in the village. Under him came the **yeomen** – richer farmers owning their own land. Then came the **tenant farmers**, who rented the lord's land. At the bottom were the **poor**, with no land. Everybody, even the poor, had a right to use the **common land** for pasture and to get firewood.

The village was a bit like a family, with the lord of the manor as 'head of the family'. In the 'manor court' of a village, the lord or his steward and a jury of the richer farmers settled any village disputes.

In the manor court, decisions were always based on **custom** – on what had happened last time a similar problem came up. The people of England respected their lords, but they also knew their rights and expected their lords to respect them.

How could the king or queen keep the nobles and the gentry on his or her side? One way was by calling a **Parliament**. The nobles and the bishops came in person to sit in the **House of Lords**. Every county and the important towns picked two **Members of Parliament (MPs)** to sit in the **House of Commons**. These MPs were local gentry or merchants.

Through Parliament, the monarch could hear the opinions of people from all over the country, and get their agreement to important changes. He or she could also ask them to vote extra **taxes** if money was needed, perhaps for a war.

Thomas Beard, an English writer, in 1597.

SOURCE

Almighty God hath appointed all things: some in high degree, some in low, some kings and princes, some inferiors and servants, masters and servants, fathers and children, husbands and wives, rich and poor.

From a sermon ordered to be read in all English churches in 1559.

SOURCE

A tenant paying rent to his lord, 1523.

SOURCE

Execution for treason, 1552. It was treason to fight or plot against the king or queen. Nobles were executed, others were tortured and hanged.

King Henry VIII in Parliament in 1523. The men sitting down are the nobles, bishops and abbots of large monasteries. The MPs of the House of Commons are at the back on the right.

A good wife should think: 'Mine husband is my superior, my better; he hath authority to rule over me; nature hath given it to him; God hath given it to him.'

William Whateley, an English clergyman, writing in 1617.

Henry VIII

Henry VIII (1491–1547) was not quite 18 when he became king in 1509. A big and handsome man, he was good at games and music, and very popular. His wife Catherine was six years older than him.

Henry wanted to increase the power of the crown and used Parliament to make the crown much more powerful. People who opposed him or got in his way were often executed for treason, including two of his wives. He encouraged artists and scholars, and had a splendid court. He fought many expensive wars, without much success. He died in 1547 aged 57. By this time he was fat and repulsive, and most people feared him.

Another way in which the monarch kept the nobles and gentry on his or her side was by **rewards** and **honours**. A nobleman might want to lead an army in war, or to go as ambassador abroad. A gentleman might want to be captain of one of the royal ships, or might want to be a **Justice of the Peace (JP)**. A JP helped to rule his part of the country. The king or queen made all these appointments. He or she also gave people honours, like a knighthood or a peerage (which made you a member of the House of Lords). So the monarch's friends and their families were likely to get the good jobs.

The nobles often came to the monarch's **court**. Here there were dances, feasts, hunting parties, processions and other events for the nobles and courtiers. But ordinary people could come to watch and admire, especially in the summer when the court moved from one palace or nobleman's house to another. So the court helped to make the king or queen popular.

1.3 The Church

In most villages in 1500 the only large building, apart from the manor house, was the **church**. Everybody helped to pay for it and the **priest** who ran it. Everybody used the church, and not just for baptisms, marriages, funerals and services on Sundays. If there was a school, it was in the church. The church organized help for the poor. People went to dance in the churchyard or to drink at church feasts, or to have their ploughs blessed, or to pray for rain. It was the centre of the village community.

The **parish church** was just a tiny part of an enormous organization. Over a group of parish priests was a **bishop**. Over a group of bishops was an **archbishop**. Over all the archbishops was the **Pope** in Rome, because the Church stretched right across Europe. The **universities**, with their libraries and learning, were part of the Church too. In earlier times, all books had been written in **Latin**, the language used by the Church. Then, hardly anyone except the **clergy** (priests, bishops and so on) could read or write. The Church was also extremely rich. With its monasteries it owned about a third of the land in England.

The monarch found this mighty organization very useful. Bishops and archbishops helped to run the country. But the Church's real power was over **people's minds**. It claimed to link all the people – from the poorest beggar to the king or queen – directly to God, the saints and the angels. Source A gives you some idea of the picture that people had in their minds. All the learned men in all the universities agreed on the general picture, although they argued about the details. **God** had made the Earth and everything in it, and watched over it all the time from heaven. But the **Devil** was at work all the time too, and people could choose his way. Some did.

A SOURCE

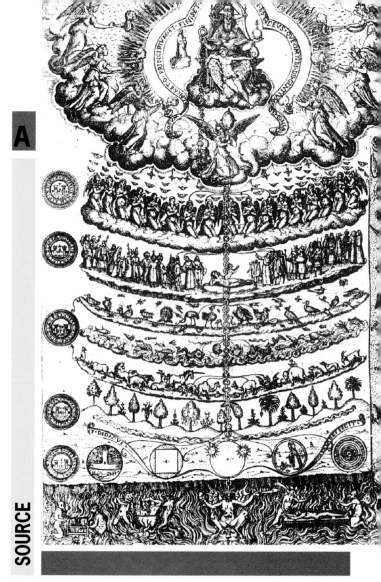

Drawing made in 1579. God is at the top, surrounded by angels. At the bottom, in hell, are the Devil and his demons, busy tormenting people. The saints are above the clouds. Below them are human beings – Europeans on the right and other people on the left. Then come birds, fishes, animals and plants in order.

B The number of witches and sorcerers has become enormous.

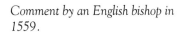

Comment by an English bishop in 1559.

C The land is full of witches. They abound in all places

Comment by an English judge in 1602.

Life for most people in 1500 was short. Accidents, disease, bad harvests or bad weather often brought disaster. Many women died in childbirth. Nobody could give any of these things a natural explanation, so everybody looked for a supernatural one. They saw spirits everywhere – good and evil – sent by God or by the Devil. Everybody believed in angels, witches, goblins and ghosts. If you followed the Devil's way you would go to hell. But the Church was God's Church and it would save you and lead you to heaven if you followed its teaching.

A witch, a warlock and a demon from hell, from a 16th-century print.

Church organization

The Pope was the earthly ruler, directly under God. When a pope died the cardinals (chief papal advisers) met and elected a new pope.

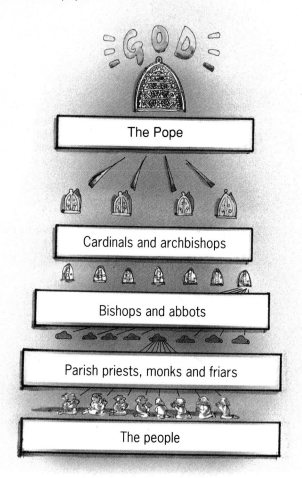

GOD

The Pope

Cardinals and archbishops

Bishops and abbots

Parish priests, monks and friars

The people

The Church.

Wolsey

Thomas Wolsey (1475?–1530) was a priest who worked for Henry VIII. Henry got the Pope to make Wolsey archbishop and cardinal, because he was so useful. As well as running the Church in England, he helped to raise taxes, to run Parliament and the law courts, and to make war and peace. Henry enjoyed being king, and was glad to leave the hard work to Wolsey. Until 1525 Wolsey was highly successful. Henry was honoured, admired and feared by English nobles and by the other rulers of Europe, including the Pope. Then things went wrong. Wolsey tried to arrange a divorce for Henry, but the Pope refused. England fought many foreign wars without success, and people blamed Wolsey – he had plenty of enemies. In 1529 Henry had him arrested for treason. He died on the way to his trial.

2.1 Henry VIII Takes Control of the Church

The first two Tudor kings, Henry VII and Henry VIII, gave England the **strong government** most people wanted. The main thing they did was to put the nobles firmly in their place. **Henry VIII** was a big man, clever and handsome (when young). People feared and admired him. He liked being in charge, and allowed nothing to stand in his way.

In about 1530 Henry had a serious problem. He and his wife Catherine had a daughter, Mary, aged 17. Catherine was too old to have any more children, and Henry was sure that only a man could keep England in order. He wanted to divorce Catherine and marry Anne Boleyn so as to have a son. The Pope refused to grant the divorce. In 1533 Henry found that Anne was pregnant. He had to act quickly and marry Anne before the child was born, so that if it was a boy, he could inherit the throne when Henry died. Henry got the Archbishop of Canterbury to grant the divorce. He quickly married Anne. This meant a split with the Pope and the Catholic Church. In 1534 Henry got Parliament to make him **Supreme Head of the Church** in England.

This greatly increased the king's **power**. As long as the Church was ruled from Rome by a foreign Pope, Henry was not fully in charge of England. Now he was. Another reason for Henry's bold action was that he was short of **money**, and the Church was very rich. The monasteries owned some of the best land in England. Once he became head of the Church, Henry **dissolved** (closed down) the monasteries, seized their land and sold it off to the nobles and gentry.

Henry's quarrel with the Pope caused another problem. At this time the Pope was trying to crush the movement known as **Protestantism** (see box). Henry disliked the Protestant ideas and wrote a book against them. But his quarrel with the Pope encouraged some English people to become Protestants. Henry tried to stop them, but without much success.

A

SOURCE

Henry VIII painted by the 16th-century artist Hans Holbein.

B

SOURCE

Sir Thomas More was a friend and adviser of Henry VIII, who appointed him Lord Chancellor. More was executed in 1535 for refusing to accept Henry as Head of the Church.

Protestants and Catholics

Martin Luther, a German monk, said that people could not be saved from hell by just going to church. To be saved, you had to believe firmly in God in your own private thoughts. Attending services in Latin which you didn't understand was no use. Services should be in people's **everyday language**, and the Church should help as many people as possible to read the Bible (God's word) for themselves. Luther and his followers were called **Protestants**. They argued that the Pope was really working for the Devil and not for God. Catholics led by the Pope argued that Protestants were **heretics**, enemies of God's true Church. The punishment for heretics was to burn them alive.

The Pilgrimage of Grace, 1536

In 1536 people from all over the north of England protested against the **dissolution of the monasteries** (as well as about taxes and corn prices). Many thousands gathered to complain. It was not quite a peaceful demonstration and not quite a rebellion. The **Duke of Norfolk**, acting for the king, promised the pilgrims that Henry would think about the complaints and would not punish them if they went home peacefully. They did this, but later over 200 of them were arrested and hanged, some in each village.

The Tudor kings and queens.

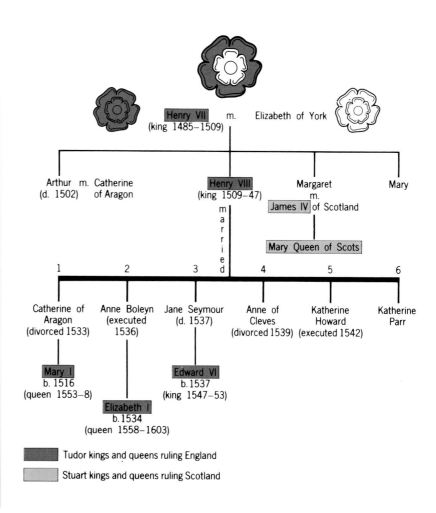

More

Sir Thomas More (1478–1535) was the son of a judge, and became a very successful lawyer himself. He became an MP and Speaker of the House of Commons. He wrote many books, including one in which he said that people should be kinder to the poor. He was interested in new ideas, and encouraged those of other writers. He was strongly opposed to the Protestant ideas of Luther, and believed firmly in the right of the Pope to rule the Church. Nearly everyone liked and admired him, including the king. Henry knighted him and gave him the important government post of Lord Chancellor in 1529.

In 1532 Henry persuaded the clergy to agree that he, rather than the Pope, was ruler of the Church. More resigned the next day in protest, although he knew that it was dangerous to oppose the king. Henry decided to get rid of More. He got Parliament to pass an act saying it was treason for anyone not to agree that the king was Head of the Church. The king's lawyers used this act to prove More was a traitor, and to condemn him to death. He was executed in 1535. He asked for help to climb up on to the scaffold, and joked that he would have no problem coming down! In 1935 the Catholic Church made him a saint.

2.2 The Tudors in Trouble

Edward VI

When Henry VIII died in 1547, his son **Edward** was only 9 years old. How could a little boy control adult men and women? How could he know who to appoint to important posts in the government or at court? How could he deal with urgent problems? There were wars with Scotland and France and a rebellion in Ireland. The court was full of ambitious nobles. Everybody was very respectful to Edward – he was now the king. But it was obvious that someone would have to rule for him until he was old enough to take control. This is exactly what happened. First the **Duke of Somerset** made himself **Lord Protector**. Then in 1551 the **Duke of Northumberland** overthrew him and took his place.

Both Protectors were keen **Protestants**. They used Parliament to take more land from the Church, and they sold it cheaply to their friends. They brought in a **new prayer book** with Protestant services, in English instead of Latin. Parliament ordered every Church to use it. In Cornwall there was a **rebellion** in 1549. Protector Somerset sent soldiers who put it down and hanged the leaders.

At this time prices were rising rapidly. Trade was bad, and harvests were poor. Many poor people were turned off their farms, and there was great **distress**. This caused another rebellion, also in 1549, this time in Norfolk. Once more, troops were sent to put it down and hang the leaders.

A

Edward VI, painted in about 1550.

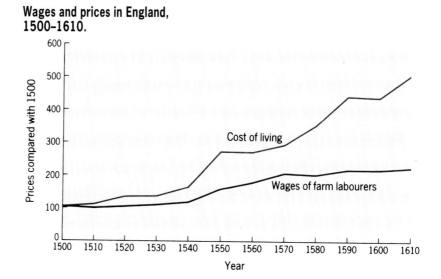

Wages and prices in England, 1500–1610.

Prices compared with 1500

Cost of living

Wages of farm labourers

Year

Mary I

In 1553 Edward died, and his sister **Mary** became queen. Mary was a devout **Catholic**. She got Parliament to bring back the Catholic services, and restored the power of the Pope in England.

At first this caused few problems. But if Mary were to keep England Catholic for ever she had to have a son to inherit the throne when she died. In 1554 she married **Philip**, son of the King of Spain. Philip, and any son they might have, would be king of both England and Spain. This would certainly keep England Catholic, as Spain was the most powerful country in Europe and very strongly Catholic.

But the English hated the idea of a foreign king. Many English people were scornful of all foreigners. They also feared that Philip (or his son if one was born) would use English money and power to do what suited Spain and not England. In 1554 a group of Kentish gentlemen marched to London to try to stop the wedding. Their rebellion failed like the rebellions of Edward's reign, and the leaders were put to death.

Mary tried to stamp out Protestant ideas in England. She and her bishops arrested Protestants who refused to give up their beliefs. They tried them for **heresy**, and burned them alive. In the years 1555–8, 300 Protestants were put to death. In 1558 Mary herself died. She had no children to carry on the Catholic faith, so the next ruler would be her half-sister **Elizabeth**, Anne Boleyn's daughter. Mary died in despair.

B

SOURCE

Thomas Cranmer, Archbishop of Canterbury 1533–55, being burned as a heretic in 1556. From a book by John Foxe, an English Protestant in exile, first published in Switzerland in 1559.

Cranmer

Thomas Cranmer (1489–1556) was a teacher at Cambridge University, who argued that the king didn't need to get the Pope's permission for a divorce. Henry employed him to spread this opinion. Cranmer was made Archbishop of Canterbury in 1532, after his support in arranging the king's divorce. He believed in new religious ideas, like the translation of the Bible into English, and allowing the clergy to marry. He was married himself. But he also believed very firmly that it was his duty to obey the king, and he always accepted Henry's policies. Under Edward VI Cranmer supported the strongly Protestant changes, and wrote many of the prayers still used in the prayer book of the Church of England.

When the Catholic Mary I became queen in 1553, she had Cranmer arrested and imprisoned him in the Tower. When her persecution of Protestants began, Cranmer lost his nerve. He signed a confession that his Protestant ideas were wrong. Mary's bishops still chose to burn him. They told him to admit his errors in public as he stood at the stake to be burned. He refused, saying that he still believed in the Protestant ideas. As the fire was lit he held out the hand that had signed the confession, to punish it by burning it first.

2.3 Two Problems for Queen Elizabeth I

Elizabeth I was 25 years old when she became Queen of England. She was lively, clever and attractive. People were delighted with their young queen. She said just the right thing to everybody, and she listened to people's advice – but then made up her own mind about what to do.

Everybody expected Elizabeth to **marry**. How could a woman keep the tough and ambitious nobles in order and lead the country both in peace and war? The only problem seemed to be, who should she choose?

Even more urgent was the problem of **religion**. Most English people had disliked the new Protestant services that were forced on them in Edward's reign. But most had been horrified to watch Protestants being burned alive by Mary. How could Elizabeth satisfy everybody?

In one way Elizabeth had no choice. She could never really accept that the Pope was right. If Henry VIII had not been right to defy the Pope and marry her mother, Elizabeth was not the lawful Queen of England. So the new Church system she and Parliament set up in 1559 had to be **Protestant** – with the Church under the queen, not under the Pope. But she made her new archbishop and bishops reject the most strongly Protestant ideas. She made them keep up as many as possible of the **old traditions**, like the clergy wearing special clothes to take services. The services were in English, but included some Catholic practices. There was to be no **persecution**, but a new law said that everybody had to go to church, and Catholics were fined for refusing.

B SOURCE

She is much attached to her people and is very sure that they love her, which is indeed true. She seems to me very much more feared than her sister, and gives her orders and has her way as completely as her father did. Everything depends on the husband she chooses, for the king's wish is obeyed here in all things. If she decides to marry out of the country she will at once fix her eyes on Your Majesty.

The Spanish Ambassador to England writing to King Philip of Spain in 1559.

C SOURCE

Elizabeth, the pretended Queen of England, has seized the place of the Supreme Head of the Church in England. We do declare her to be deprived of her pretended title. We do command all noblemen and people not to obey her or her orders.

An order issued by the Pope in 1570.

A SOURCE

Elizabeth dancing at court with Robert Dudley, Earl of Leicester.

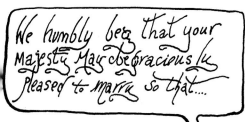

During Elizabeth's long reign of 45 years, ordinary people got used to this system. The schools and universities produced a new generation of educated people who had never known anything else. So Elizabeth's new **'Church of England'** was very successful. It still exists.

Some people objected. Many Protestants thought far too much was being kept of the old system. These **Puritans** (see box) accepted Elizabeth's Church but hoped to change it slowly. Many Catholics, especially in the north of England, stayed faithful to the Pope and the old religion. But as time went on, most English people came to hate and fear the Pope and these 'Papists'. This was partly because of books like that of John Foxe (page 13, Source B). But it was mainly because in 1570 the Pope issued orders that Elizabeth was to be deposed from the throne, and he asked Catholic countries like Spain to invade England and overthrow the queen. This made all Catholics look like traitors. Parliament made it treason for Catholics to convert English people to the Catholic faith. Many priests who did were tortured and executed.

Leicester

Robert Dudley, Earl of Leicester, (1532?–88) was a nobleman at Elizabeth I's court. He was tall and handsome and just two years older than Elizabeth. They often went dancing and hunting together. In 1560 Dudley's wife, Amy, was found dead. People said she had been murdered so he could marry the queen. In fact she had probably committed suicide.

Elizabeth may well have loved Dudley, but she knew that if she married an English noble all the others would be jealous. In any case, Amy's suspicious death made it quite impossible.

Dudley remained a trusted adviser to the queen and she made him Earl of Leicester. Later, he married one of the ladies of the court. Courtiers were expected to ask the queen's permission to marry, and Elizabeth was furious that Dudley had not done this. She eventually forgave him. In 1585 he led an English army to help the Dutch to fight against Spain, but with little success. He served the queen loyally until his death in 1588.

The Puritans

Many strict Protestants wanted plain and simple church services, so that nothing could distract people from listening to the minister or from praying. The Church's job was just to teach people, and to lead the fight against sin. It should put a stop to anything that might encourage sin. This included dancing round the maypole, drinking at Church feasts, holding Christmas parties, even going to the theatre or wearing brightly coloured clothes. These **Puritans** thought only God could choose who to save from hell, and the churches should be run by the men God had clearly chosen: themselves.

Mary Queen of Scots

In 1562 **Queen Elizabeth** had smallpox and nearly died. If she had died, then the person with the best claim to the throne would have been her cousin, **Mary Queen of Scots**. But Mary had been brought up as a French princess and was a devout Catholic. If she became Queen of England there would probably be yet another complete change of religion. Elizabeth soon recovered, but Mary's chances still looked good. All she had to do was wait. She was nine years younger than Elizabeth; even more important, she had a son, **James**, born in 1566.

In 1568 a **rebellion** broke out in Scotland against Mary. It was partly about religion. Protestantism was spreading strongly in Scotland, and the nobles and Church leaders had set up their own Protestant 'Church of Scotland'. But the murder of Mary's husband actually started the rebellion. The Scots believed that Mary had planned the killing. Soon afterwards she married the **Earl of Bothwell**, who had probably arranged the murder.

Elizabeth sent troops to help the Scots lords, and warships to stop France helping Mary's supporters in Scotland. Mary was overthrown and she fled across the border into England, leaving her baby son behind. The rebel lords accepted him as **King James VI** of Scotland and carefully educated him as a Protestant.

What was Elizabeth do to with Mary? If she handed her back to the Scots, they would put her to death for the murder. Elizabeth was horrified at the very thought of people executing their own queen, and her cousin too! But if Mary came to court she might soon find plenty of friends among the nobles. Mary was lively and attractive. She had already had three husbands and had been queen of two countries, though she was still only 25 years old. English nobles who were discontented or just ambitious might offer to help her take the throne. So might the King of France, the King of Spain, or the Pope.

Elizabeth decided that it was safest to keep Mary as a captive in the north of England, though with full honour as a queen. Even here, over the next 20 years, Mary was the centre of a series of plots (see box).

A

SOURCE

A 16th-century portrait of Mary Queen of Scots, aged between 16 and 18.

The northern rebellion, 1569
Many people in the north of England were still Catholic at heart. Also the nobles there wanted more power for themselves. The plan was to seize Mary, march to London and force Elizabeth to dismiss her Protestant advisers and restore the old religion. But Elizabeth sent troops, who defeated the rebels fairly easily and hanged 800 of them.

The Ridolfi plot, 1571
This was a plot to overthrow Elizabeth, marry Mary to the Duke of Norfolk, the leading English noble, and place her on the throne. The Pope and the King of Spain promised to help. Elizabeth's government heard about the plot, and it collapsed. Norfolk was executed as a traitor.

The Throckmorton plot, 1583
Throckmorton was a Catholic gentleman. He took letters from Mary to the Spanish Ambassador. English Catholics planned to rebel and Spain was to send help to them. Elizabeth's spies found out, and Throckmorton and others were executed.

The Babington plot, 1586
Babington and other Catholic gentlemen planned to kill the queen and put Mary on the throne. He wrote to Mary to get her agreement. But Elizabeth's spies were watching him. They had cracked his code and were reading all his and Mary's letters. When Mary replied and agreed to the plan, they arrested Babington and his friends. Now they had the evidence they needed to act against Mary too.

The execution of Mary Queen of Scots in 1587 – a drawing made by a Dutch artist soon after the event.

Finally, in 1586 Elizabeth's spies had clear evidence that Mary had taken part in **Babington**'s plan to murder her. So Elizabeth set up a court to try her cousin. Mary was found guilty.

Elizabeth tried everything to avoid signing the death warrant. To execute a queen seemed to be against God. But in the end, in 1587, she signed. Her advisers and the whole of Protestant England breathed an enormous sigh of relief.

Walsingham

Sir Francis Walsingham (1530?–90) was Elizabeth's Secretary of State. He was an expert on foreign policy and organized spies for the queen. He hated and feared Catholics, including the rulers of France and Spain. He was completely loyal to Elizabeth, and she listened to his expert advice, but always made up her own mind what to do.

Walsingham found out about plots against the queen. He helped the Babington plotters to send secret messages to Mary Queen of Scots. Barrels of beer were regularly sent to Mary and her servants in the castle where she was imprisoned. Secret messages going in and out were wrapped in waterproof covers and put inside the barrels. Walsingham read them, and collected clear evidence that Mary had agreed to the plot to kill Elizabeth. Walsingham was ill when Elizabeth signed Mary's death warrant in 1587, so William Davison, another secretary, sent it off. Elizabeth said afterwards that she had not really meant to send it, and she sent Davison to the Tower.

It would have been better to have poisoned her or to have choked her with a pillow, but not to put her to so open a death.

SOURCE

A Spanish nobleman commenting on the execution of Mary in 1587.

2.5 War With Spain

In 1588 **King Philip II of Spain** tried to invade England. He wanted to force Elizabeth off the throne. Why did Philip attack? Why did he fail?

Catholics and Protestants

In the later 16th century, bitter **wars** between Protestants and Catholics divided the continent of Europe (see map).

King Philip II, the leader of Catholic Europe, ruled many parts of Europe, as well as Spain (see map). In the Netherlands, the Protestants were rebelling against him. In 1585 Elizabeth sent an English army to help the rebels. Philip also had an empire in **America** and the **Far East**. He was the most powerful ruler in the world.

A

SOURCE

Queen Elizabeth I, painted to celebrate the defeat of the Spanish Armada in 1588.

Western Europe in 1588, showing the route taken by the Spanish Armada.

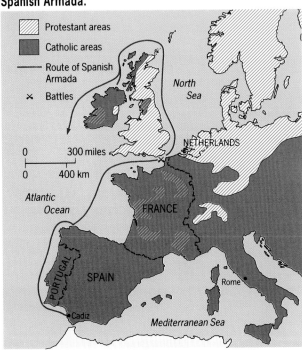

The Atlantic and the Americas in Elizabeth I's reign.

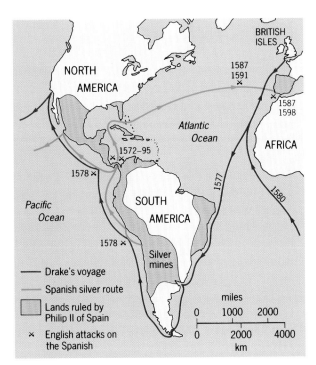

The sea-dogs

The Spanish and the Portuguese were the first Europeans to conquer the **newly discovered lands** in America and the Far East. In America they found rich **silver** mines, and every year a fleet of ships brought the silver to Spain. The Spanish wanted to keep all foreigners out so as to keep the silver and the trade in their own hands. **English sailors** wanted a share, and in the 1570s they began to attack Spanish trading posts and ships in America. They were known as 'sea-dogs'. **Francis Drake**, a poor Devon gentleman, made his fortune by doing this. London merchants were glad to lend money to Drake and other sea-dogs. In 1577–80 Drake sailed right around the world, attacking Spanish ships as he went. People who had shared the cost of Drake's voyage got back 47 times as much money as they had put in. One of them was Queen Elizabeth.

The Armada campaign

In 1588 Philip attacked with the **Spanish Armada,** a fleet of 130 ships carrying 30,000 men. It was to sail to the Netherlands, join with another army of 30,000, land near Margate and take control of England.

The English made their big attack while the Armada was waiting near Calais to link up with the Spanish army from the Netherlands. The English had 135 ships but the ones which won the battle were 24 warships of a new design, developed by the sea-dogs. These warships had heavy cannon which could be fired again and again to smash up enemy ships. The Spanish had good guns, but hardly used them. Their ships were designed to go alongside an enemy ship and use soldiers to board it. The Spanish fleet didn't stand a chance. Only three of their ships were sunk; the rest fled. Many were so badly damaged that about 40 were wrecked in storms on the way home. No English ships were lost.

The war after the Armada

England went on helping the **Dutch** Protestants in the Netherlands. They became an independent nation. The Spanish sent help to Catholics in **Ireland** who were rebelling against Elizabeth. The English went on attacking Spanish ships and ports, but were never able to cut off the silver route altogether. By 1604 both Elizabeth and Philip were dead, and the two countries made peace.

Drake

Sir Francis Drake (1540?–96) was a sailor from Devon who traded with Africa and the Spanish Empire in America. This was against Spanish law. In 1567 he only just escaped when many of his friends were captured by the Spaniards. He got his own back by raiding Panama in 1572. The silver he seized made him rich, and brought him to the queen's notice. She liked his boldness, and agreed to his famous voyage round the world. On the way, Drake captured many Spanish ships and seized their rich cargoes. The Spanish were furious, but the queen knighted him when got back.

Drake and other British sailors at that time worked out a new style of sea fighting. This was one of the main reason for the success of the English against the Spanish. In 1587 Drake led a successful raid on the naval port of Cadiz in Spain, and in 1588 he led some ships against the Armada. Drake made other raids on Spanish America, but the Spaniards had improved their defences; these later attacks did not cause much damage. It was on one of these raids, in 1595, that he was taken ill and died.

3.1 England Gets Richer

Trade

The two maps below show one of the most important changes in British and world history. Between 1480 and 1600 European ships sailed to most parts of the world. Europeans became worldwide traders. Spain and Portugal took the lead, but England soon joined in.

Industry

England had plenty of goods to **export**. English industries grew in step with English trade. By far the most important was the making of **woollen cloth**. By 1600 cloth made in Yorkshire and Norfolk was sold as far away as Russia and India.

The world known to Europeans in about 1480.

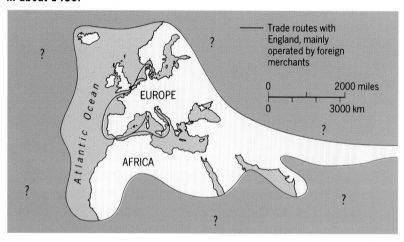

The world known to Europeans by about 1600.

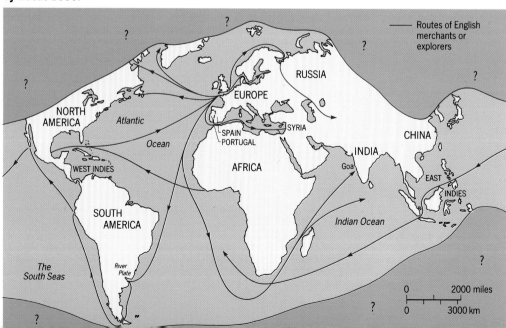

A

SOURCE

The opinion of our ships among foreigners is that for strength, nimbleness and swiftness of sailing there are no vessels in the world to be compared with ours.

From William Harrison, 'Description of England', 1587.

B

SOURCE

None of the kings of this land before Her Majesty had English consuls at Tripoli in Syria or at Babylon. Who ever heard of Englishmen at Goa [India] before now? What English ships did ever before now anchor in the mighty River Plate [South America], cross the breadth of the South Sea and return home richly laden with goods from China, as the subjects of this flourishing monarchy have done?

From Richard Hakluyt, 'Principal Navigations of the English Nation', 1589.

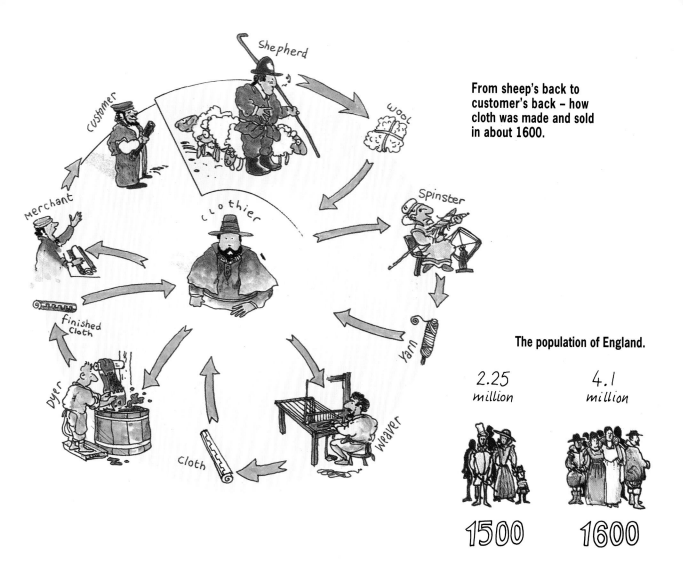

From sheep's back to customer's back – how cloth was made and sold in about 1600.

Shepherd
Wool
Spinster
Yarn
Weaver
Cloth
Dyer
finished Cloth
Merchant
customer
clothier

The population of England.

2.25 million	4.1 million
1500	1600

Jenkinson

Anthony Jenkinson (1525?–1611) was an English merchant and sailor. As a young man he traded with all the countries around the Mediterranean Sea and got permission from the sultan of Turkey to trade there. In 1557 he was sent to Russia by the Muscovy Company, London merchants who were opening up a new trade route to Russia, north of Norway. Jenkinson landed in northern Russia in July. Travelling by river boat and sledge he got to Moscow in December. He saw the tsar of Russia and got permission to travel farther. In 1558 he went by river to the Caspian Sea, then by camel through the desert to Bokhara, Central Asia. He was attacked by thieves and local chieftains on the way, and shipwrecked on the Caspian Sea.

But he overcame all these difficulties, partly because he and his party had guns and the locals had none. Bokhara was a centre for trade with China, India and Persia (Iran). Jenkinson studied the trade there, and sold some cloth which he had brought from England. After more adventures he returned to London in 1560 and wrote a detailed report of the trip. He made several other journeys to Russia. Jenkinson also wrote a report for the queen on the idea of sailing all the way round the north of Russia to China, and advised her on Frobisher's attempt to sail to China round the north of Canada.

Jenkinson married, had ten children (four died young) and was very rich.

London and the Thames, looking northwards across London Bridge, late 16th century.

FLUVIUS

South Warke

SOURCE

Peace and prosperity

During the 16th century, the strong rule of the Tudor kings and queens brought **peace** in England. There were several rebellions, but they were all put down quite easily with very little fighting. There were several **foreign wars**, but the fighting took place in Scotland or Ireland, on the Continent (Europe) or at sea. So English people could grow food, and make and sell cloth and other goods, in peace.

London

London was the centre of England's new wealth. **Transport** was easy on the Thames or by coastal ships to and from all parts of the country and the Continent. Between 1500 and 1600 London's **population** shot up from 50,000 to 200,000. **Farmers** in the nearby counties grew and sold far more to feed all the extra people. New **industries** developed (see Source D); and the old industries, like shipbuilding on the Thames, expanded. The iron foundries of Sussex supplied cannon for the ships and fire-irons for people's houses. The changes in London changed the whole of **south-east England**.

In the **north** the new trade and the new industry caused less change. But as well as the Yorkshire cloth industry, there was **coal mining** around Newcastle. Ships and seamen were needed to carry the coal to London. (London people called it 'sea coale'.)

D

There is a great scarcity of wood. The Londoners have to make their fires of sea coale even in the chambers of rich persons. They have of late discovered the making of glass and the burning of brick with sea coale.

SOURCE

From John Stow, 'Annals', 1605.

E

London is a mighty city of business. Most men work in trade. The river is most convenient. Ships from other kingdoms come up almost to the city. The inhabitants are magnificently dressed and are extremely proud. They care little for foreigners, but scoff and laugh at them.

SOURCE

Written by a German visitor in 1592.

Gresham

Sir Thomas Gresham (1519?–79) was a London merchant. He traded in many things, but was an expert in buying and selling foreign money, and borrowing money for the government. He had spies and agents all over Europe, and acted as adviser to Henry VIII, Edward VI, Mary I and Elizabeth I. He helped Elizabeth to improve the English coinage. The Tudor monarchs paid well, but he also made a profit for himself. He owned an iron foundry and a paper mill. He invested money in overseas exploration. He founded a college in London to teach subjects useful to trade. He died in 1579, leaving most of his wealth to charity, but over £2000 a year to his widow (worth £600,000 today).

Sutton

Thomas Sutton (1532–1611) was a soldier. While serving in the north of England he bought and rented coal mines which supplied London. He became very rich, moved to London and became even richer by lending money at interest. At one time, six earls owed him money. He was said to be the richest person in England not counting nobles, and he was actually much richer than most of them. When he died in 1611 he left over £60,000 (mostly money lent out at interest; about £18,000,000 today), and land worth £5000 a year (about £1,500,000 today). He founded a hospital and a school. The school still exists. He had a son, but he left all his money to charity. Later the law courts gave his son a share.

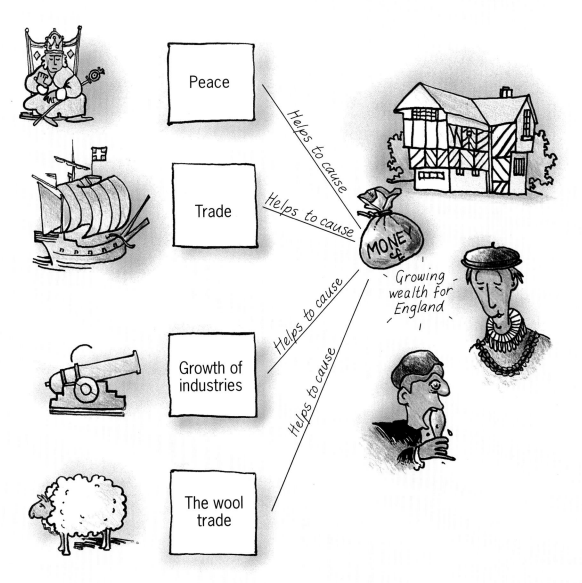

Peace

Trade

Growth of industries

The wool trade

Helps to cause

Helps to cause

Helps to cause

Helps to cause

MONEY £

Growing wealth for England

3.2 The Poor Get Poorer

Although England as a whole got much richer in the 16th and 17th centuries, it was a bad time for the **poor**. This was partly because of a **rise in prices.** Food prices went up twice as fast as wages; so anybody who relied on wages for a living was much worse off. In the villages where most people lived, the poor often had a tiny patch of land to grow food, and could keep a few animals on the **common**. But other changes were happening in the villages, as you can see in the cartoon. The main change was **enclosure**: the lords or richer farmers fenced off the common or part of it into private fields. Poor people found they could no longer make a living in their own village, and many roamed the country looking for work.

Parliament passed many laws to try to stop enclosure. But the landowners who were enclosing the commons were often the JPs who were supposed to enforce the law. So the laws never worked.

The Poor Law

Everybody was worried about the poor, from the king or queen down to the poor people themselves. Some beggars turned to crime or violence. People were often frightened if they saw a gang of ragged strangers coming along the road.

By 1601 Parliament had built up a new **Poor Law** which lasted for over 200 years. It was based on the village church, the natural place where the poor of the parish expected help from their richer neighbours. The people who ran the Poor Law in each village, the **churchwardens**, were the richer village people themselves. They did help the old, the sick and the orphans in their own villages. But they thought that all able-bodied poor people were just idlers and they treated them harshly.

The Poor Law, 1601

- Each **parish** to look after its own poor.
- The **churchwardens** to collect a fair **poor rate** from every landowner.
- Churchwardens to help the poor people of their own village who were poor through **no fault of their own**.
- People who were poor because they were **idle** were to be whipped and made to work or sent to prison.
- **Beggars from other villages** to be whipped and sent home.

SOURCE A

Noblemen and gentlemen enclose all into pasture. They throw down houses. The poor people be forced out, or else by wrongs and injuries they be compelled to sell all. By one means or another they must depart away, poor wretched souls. Men, women, fatherless children, widows, woeful mothers with their young babes – away they trudge. All their household stuff, which is worth very little, they be forced to sell for hardly anything. And when they have wandered about till they have spent that, what can they do but steal, and then be hanged, or go about begging?

From Sir Thomas More, 'Utopia', 1516. More was a leading lawyer.

SOURCE B

Every rogue, vagabond or sturdy beggar shall be stripped naked from the middle upwards and shall be openly whipped until his or her back be bloody, and sent the direct way to the parish where he was born.

An Act of Parliament of 1597.

SOURCE C

Paid for thatching old Margaret Bothom's house – two shillings.
Paid to Henry Bradshaw when his wife gave birth – a shilling.
Paid for mending widow Chamley's shoes – 10 pence.

17th-century Poor Law accounts from Glossop in Derbyshire.

SOURCE D

One way of treating poor people in England in 1577.

Beggars

Few people wrote about the poor. We have only a few lines from poor-law accounts or court records. Here are some examples.

1548 *Robert Shakesbury*, a child: whipped and sent out of London for pretending to have a disease which made his body shake.

1577 *Katherine Frank*: sent to prison for sleeping in the streets under market stalls.

1580 *Elizabeth Whalley*, a pregnant woman: given 12 pence, and ordered to go home to Norwich. Found sleeping in London streets.

1582 *Thomas and Isabell Wylde*, peddlers: arrested for begging in Warwick on their way from Settle, Yorkshire, to London.

1598 *Joan Wood*: arrested for begging while visiting her son in Leicester prison to bring him food and 2 pence in cash.

1635 *Ellen Dixon*, a blind woman: whipped and set in the stocks in Windermere for begging without a licence.

1633 *John Sheppard*: went off leaving his wife and six small children in Bedfordshire. The wife died, leaving the children with nothing.

1640 *William Clay*, a man with no legs: sent to prison and put to work making gloves, for begging without a licence.

THE MAKING OF THE UK 25

3.3 England and Britain

The London area

In the 16th century, the **south-east of England** – the area around London – acted like a magnet pulling the whole of the British Isles much closer together. London grew as a centre of **trade and industry**. The strong Tudor kings and queens and their Parliaments made rules that applied to the whole country and saw that they were enforced.

London was also the main centre for publishing **books**, so the way Londoners spelled and wrote became accepted as '**standard English**'. Nobles, gentry and merchants from all over England often came to London. They spoke their own local dialects but they wrote and read in London English. Shakespeare wrote his plays in it. The new Bibles and prayerbooks that had to be used in all churches carried London English all over the country, and to Ireland and Scotland.

The north and the west

The **north** and the **west** of England were much poorer than the south-east. New ideas spread more slowly there, and there were several **rebellions** against changes ordered from London. But most people wanted good order and strong government, so they supported the Crown, and the rebellions were put down fairly easily. Industry and trade helped. Cornish tin-miners, Devon sailors or Yorkshire cloth-merchants brought wealth to these areas. Also, success in the war against Spain made Queen Elizabeth popular everywhere.

Wales

The Tudors were partly Welsh, and this helped them to bring Wales under full control. Parliament passed Acts in 1536 and 1543 to divide Wales into counties like the English ones, and to apply all English laws to Wales. This suited the Welsh nobles and gentry. They could now become JPs and MPs or get jobs for themselves or their sons at court or in London – provided they learned English. Like the English gentry they were keen to buy **monastery lands** from Henry VIII. They accepted Elizabeth's moderate **Protestant Church**. Most of the poorer people went on speaking Welsh and feeling Welsh, but they had lost their leaders.

Scotland

Scotland and **England** were old enemies, but the events of Elizabeth's reign brought them together. Protestantism had

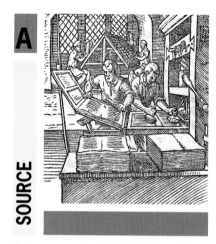

A SOURCE

Printers at work. By 1600 about 200 books a year were being published in England; others were brought in from abroad. Most gentlemen, but hardly any women, could read. About one man in five could read – more in London.

B

They rejected these designs:

They used this one:

SOURCE

Early Union Flags for the warships of King James I of Great Britain; two rejected designs and the successful one.

Jesus College, Oxford, founded in 1571, mainly for Welsh students. Oxford and Cambridge were the only universities in England or Wales. During the 16th century it became usual for the sons of the gentry to go there. Some yeomen's sons went too, but no women.

No persons that use the Welsh speech shall have any manner of office or fees within this realm.

An Act of Parliament of 1536.

Stratford-on-Avon Grammar School, founded in 1548. Shakespeare was probably a pupil here in the 1570s. Gentlemen, yeomen and merchants mostly sent their sons (not their daughters) to school.

spread to Scotland and to England at the same time. When the Scots rebelled against Mary Queen of Scots and made Scotland Protestant, Elizabeth sent help. So there was a strong English influence in Scotland when King James VI (Mary's son) was growing up. When the Church of Scotland produced a new translation of the Bible in 1580 it was written in London (not Scots) English. James knew that he had by far the best claim to inherit the English throne if Elizabeth died, so he kept friendly relations with Elizabeth's ministers and nobles. When Elizabeth died in 1603 most English people were delighted to welcome him as **King James I of England**.

King James I ruled Scotland from England and this helped the two nations to mix. Scots nobles and gentry came to court. Shakespeare wrote a play about Scotland, *Macbeth*. Scots read English books. Scots and English merchants traded with each other. But many Scots and English people still distrusted and disliked each other. James wanted to unify his two kingdoms completely, but the English Parliament refused. However, James did change his own title. In 1604 he announced that he was **King of Great Britain**.

Shakespeare

William Shakespeare (1564–1616) was the son of a merchant in Stratford-on-Avon. He went to London when he was 24 years old. He became an actor, poet and theatre-owner, and wrote at least 36 plays.

No other writer of English has ever been so admired. Phrases from his plays and poems soon became part of the language, making it more expressive. His understanding of human feelings and character have appealed to people all over the world.

Shakespeare became very rich and retired to Stratford in 1611.

Ireland

It was very hard for the English to bring **Ireland** under control from London. The English nobles in Ireland often rebelled. Many of them spoke Irish as well as English and could get help from Irish friends and relations. In spite of this Henry VIII was quite successful there. He persuaded the nobles to agree to his break from the Pope – they were quite glad to buy monastery lands from him. In 1541 the Irish Parliament even changed Henry's title to **King of Ireland** instead of 'Lord'. But this made no real difference to Henry's power over the nobles. There were still many rebellions.

In the 1550s the English adopted a new plan – **plantation**. They sent a much larger army to Ireland. To pay for it they seized the land of Irish rebels and sold it to settlers from England. The idea was that these settlers would bring the English language and laws to Ireland. Backed up by a strong army, this would bring Ireland under firm control.

It was at this time that religion became an important cause of trouble between England and Ireland. Elizabeth had set up the Protestant Church of England. So the English settlers of her reign were Protestants. All churches in Ireland were ordered to use the English Bible and prayer book. Now Catholics in Ireland had a new reason to rebel.

The Catholic Irish also had a new source of help – **Philip II of Spain**. But Elizabeth sent a larger army than ever before, backed up by the warships which had beaten the Spanish Armada. By the time of her death in 1603, English armies and navies were completely in control of the whole of Ireland for the first time.

James I began his reign with the **plantation of Ulster**, just 20 miles across the sea from Scotland. Many Scots Protestants had already settled there. In Ulster lived the toughest Irish rebels, the O'Neills. In 1607 their lands were seized. The English and Scots people who settled there in the following 20 years or so are the ancestors of the present-day Protestants of Northern Ireland. But not far from their settlements, living on the worst land, or working as labourers for the settlers, were Catholic Irish people, full of bitter memories and fear and hatred of the settlers who had taken their land.

SOURCE F

All English even in Dublin speak Irish, and are greatly spotted in manners, dress and conditions with Irish stains.

The view of an English official in 1578.

SOURCE G

Sir Humphrey Gilbert ordered that the heads of those which were killed should be cut off and brought to the place where he camped, and laid by each side of the way into his own tent. Nobody could come to his tent without passing through a lane of heads.

From an account of the fighting in Ireland. It was written in 1575 by Thomas Churchyard, an English writer who fought in the English army.

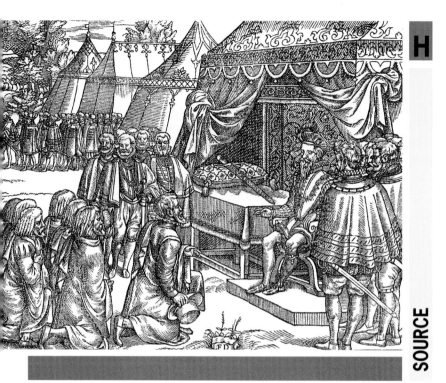

H

SOURCE

From an English book of 1581. An Irish Lord accepts the authority of Elizabeth's Lord Deputy in Ireland (sitting down) in 1575.

Tyrone

Hugh O'Neill, the Earl of Tyrone, (1540?–1616) was an Irish nobleman. He came to the court of Elizabeth I, and was educated as an English lord. When he went back to Ireland he was, for a time, on the side of the English against Irish rebellions. But he was still the leader of his clan and still spoke Irish.

As the policy of plantation continued, more and more English Protestants settled in Ireland. Religious bitterness increased. O'Neill led a rebellion in Ulster against the English Protestants. He hoped that Catholic Spain might help Catholic Ireland to throw out the English. He won a battle against the English and, in 1601, a Spanish army landed at Kinsale (see map) to help. But O'Neill was not a good general, and often quarrelled with the other Irish leaders. The English drove out the Spanish and suppressed the rebellion, and O'Neill made peace with them. He even came to London to the court of King James I. Later, however, new quarrels broke out in Ireland, and O'Neill heard of a secret English plan to arrest him for treason. So he decided to change sides again. In 1607, he and several other Irish lords fled from Ireland to Rome. Here he died in 1616. James I confiscated his land and used it for the plantation of Ulster.

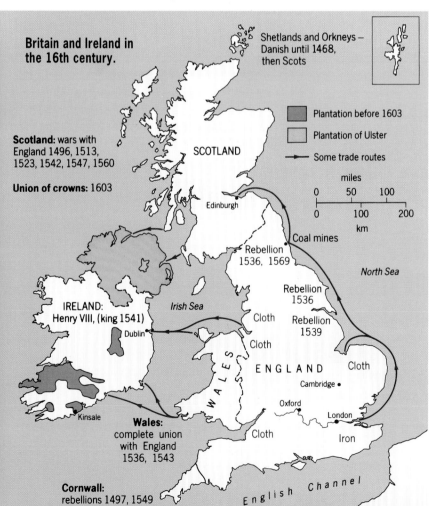

Britain and Ireland in the 16th century.

Shetlands and Orkneys – Danish until 1468, then Scots

Scotland: wars with England 1496, 1513, 1523, 1542, 1547, 1560

Union of crowns: 1603

SCOTLAND

Edinburgh

Plantation before 1603

Plantation of Ulster

Some trade routes

miles
0   50   100

0   100   200
km

Rebellion 1536, 1569

Coal mines

North Sea

IRELAND: Henry VIII, (king 1541)

Irish Sea

Dublin

Rebellion 1536

Rebellion 1539

Cloth

Cloth

Cloth

W A L E S

E N G L A N D

Cloth

Cambridge •

Oxford •

London •

Kinsale

Wales: complete union with England 1536, 1543

Cloth

Iron

Cornwall: rebellions 1497, 1549

English Channel

3.4 People and Houses

Until about 1500 most houses in Britain were made of wood and had roofs of thatch. Hardly any are left for us to see, since these materials easily rot. Also a great many were **rebuilt** during the 16th and 17th centuries in lasting materials like stone, brick, slate and tiles. Hundreds of these new houses are still in use today all over the country. The cartoon suggests some of the reasons why this important change took place.

The queen keeps good peace in England now. This damp old castle is no use any more.

Every year we do better, husband! 'Tis time we pulled down our smokey house and built a better one, with one of those chimneys and walls of stone.

Glass windows in a house; it's like a church! What a good idea - they let the light in and keep the wind out.

No stone near here and oak costs far too much. But now we've got plenty of bricks.

The lands of Woburn Abbey would join nicely on to my estate. Now the king has made me Earl of Bedford, I need the sort of house fit for my title.

What magnificent style! When I get home I must copy these Italian buildings.

Bess of Hardwick

Elizabeth Hardwick (1518–1607), the Countess of Shrewsbury, had four husbands, each richer than the one before. Beautiful, witty, clever and completely determined, she made sure that most of the wealth of all four went to the six children of her third husband.

Bess organized the building of several great houses, and ran large estates, including lead and coal mines. She quarrelled with her fourth husband, because of his friendship with Mary Queen of Scots, a prisoner in their castle. She also quarrelled with Queen Elizabeth and spent a short time in the Tower. She died in 1607 aged 89.

The royal palaces

Kings and queens had several palaces. The court included hundreds of nobles and other attendants. So a palace needed great halls for official meetings and feasts, dances, music and plays. It needed kitchens and store-rooms, stables and places for servants to sleep. It was very important for the king or queen to impress foreign ambassadors as well as British nobles with how rich, successful and up-to-date the crown and the court were.

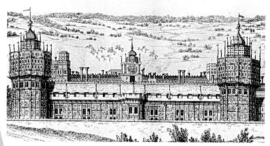

Nonsuch Palace, Surrey, built by Henry VIII.

Hardwick Hall, Derbyshire, built by Elizabeth, the Countess of Shrewsbury, in 1597.

The great houses of the nobles

Nobles had to impress people too. The gentry from the whole county often came to the nobleman's '**great house**'. There were hunting parties, weddings and funerals. The local gentry came to ask favours or to talk politics or business. There had to be room for 50 or 60 people, family, servants and visitors. If the house was within about 100 miles of London, the king or queen might come to stay. This was such an honour that people built extra rooms, to give the right impression.

The gentleman's house

The **country gentleman** needed a large hall so that all the village people could crowd in to a party at Christmas. He might hold the manor court there, or sit there as a JP to deal with criminals. But he needed comfortable private rooms too, each with a modern fireplace, for his family and his friends. If he hoped to be chosen as MP by the other gentry and the yeomen of the county, he had be hospitable to them and their wives.

Little Moreton Hall, Cheshire.

A late 16th-century yeoman's house in Edwardstone, Suffolk.

The yeoman's house

A rich **yeoman** might be better off than a poor gentleman, because yeomen had fewer expenses, and no need to show off. But yeomen did want to be comfortable, and they could afford it. Many rebuilt their houses in lasting materials. They had proper fireplaces in two or three of the rooms, glass in the windows and plenty of food on the solid oak table.

The houses of the tenant farmers and the poor

We know far less about these houses, because few, if any, still exist. A tenant farmer did not own his farm himself, so he did not rebuild the house. He just repaired the thatch or the walls, and perhaps built a fireplace and chimney at one end. We can only guess about the cottages of the **poor**. We do know that the poor got poorer, so their houses probably became damper, draughtier and more unhealthy. Finally there were many **wandering beggars** who had no houses at all.

4.1 The Gunpowder Plot

On **5 November 1605** King James I was due to open his first Parliament. The lords and all the MPs would be crowded into the House of Lords to hear him speak. On the evening of 4 November a mysterious message was passed to Lord Mounteagle. He was a Catholic, and the letter advised him not to go to Parliament. He showed it **Robert Cecil**, James's chief adviser, and Cecil sent soldiers to search the Parliament building.

In the cellar under the House of Lords they found 36 barrels of gunpowder, and **Guy Fawkes**, a Catholic Yorkshireman, getting the fuse ready to light when Parliament met. The plotters' idea was to seize the king's children, put one of them on the throne and make England Catholic again. The plotters were put on trial and executed for treason.

Fawkes

Guy Fawkes (1570–1606) was the son of a York lawyer. His father, a Protestant, died when Fawkes was 9 years old. His mother then married a Catholic. So he grew up in a Catholic family when Elizabeth was at war with Spain – a time when Catholic priests were hunted down as traitors. When he was 21 years old Fawkes inherited his father's property, sold it and went to the Netherlands. In 1593 he became a soldier in the Spanish army, fighting against the Protestant Dutch and their English allies. He was just the man the Gunpowder Plotters needed. He was brave, determined and had a knowledge of gunpowder. He probably had no idea how little support the plotters had for their plan – most English Catholics knew nothing about it and were horrified when they found out.

Fawkes showed great courage when he was found out. When the first officials looked into the cellar on 4 November and spoke to him, he thought they hadn't noticed the gunpowder, so he stayed on to get the fuse ready. When he was arrested he boldly admitted the plan to kill the king, and only gave the names of the others after torture and when some of them were captured.

A SOURCE

Guy Fawkes on his way to set the fuse on the night of November 4 1605 – a cartoon drawn soon afterwards.

my lord out of the loue i beare to some of youere freindz i haue a caer of youer preseruacion therfor i woulcd aduyse yowe as yowbe Tender youer lyf to deuys some expcuse to shift of youer attendance at this parleament for god and man hathe concurred to punishe the wickednes of this tyme and thinke not sleightly of this aduertisment but retyere youre self into youre contri whear youe maye expect the euent in safti for thowghe theare be no apparance of anni stir yet i saye they shall receyue a terrible blowe this parleament and yet they shall not seie who hurts them this convncel is not to be contemned because it maye do yowe good and can do yowe no harme for the dangere is passed as soon as youe haue burnt the letter and i hope god will giue yowe the grace to mak good use of it to whose holy proteccion i comend yowe

To the ryght honorable
The lord mounteagle

The letter sent to Lord Mounteagle on 4 November 1605.

Protestant England rejoiced that the dreadful **gunpowder plot** had failed. Pamphlets were written and sermons were preached about it. 5 November became a date which most English people celebrated with bonfires which renewed their fear and hatred of the Pope.

There are **two theories** about the plot. Historians agree that the gunpowder was there and that Fawkes was arrested as he was getting things ready for the explosion the next day. The **first theory** is that Robert Cecil only found out just in time, from the mysterious message. The **second theory** is that he knew about the plot beforehand through spies, and allowed Fawkes and his friends to go ahead. He even made it easy for them to get gunpowder from a government store, so that he could catch them red-handed.

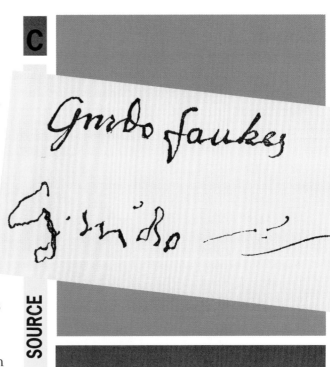

Fawkes's signature before and after torture.

4.2 1603–40: What Went Wrong?

Under the Tudor kings and queens, most people in England were delighted to have **strong government**. Queen Elizabeth I was probably the most popular ruler in all English history. But in 1640, only 37 years after her death, a Parliament set about cutting down the power of the king, and this caused a **civil war**. What turned king and Parliament against each other?

The kings' favourites and advisers

King James I and his son **Charles I** were no good at keeping the leading nobles and gentry on their side, as Elizabeth had done so well. From 1618 to 1628 the chief minister was **George Villiers, Duke of Buckingham**. James promoted him over the heads of all the older nobles, mainly because of his good looks.

Buckingham made sure that all the king's favours and all the worthwhile jobs went to his own friends and relatives. He did try to make himself popular by joining in wars on the Continent; but the attacks he led on Spain in 1625 and on France in 1627 were both flops. This made him more unpopular than ever. In 1628 he was murdered by a discontented army officer.

After Buckingham's death, Charles I's main advisers were **William Laud, Archbishop of Canterbury**, and **Thomas Wentworth, Earl of Strafford**, who ruled the north of England and Ireland for the king. Laud and Strafford believed that Britain needed strong and determined government. If anyone got in the way of this, so much the worse for them! By 1640 they had made enemies in all three kingdoms.

James I was a clever man who often annoyed people with his sharp remarks. Although he looks dignified here, he really wasn't.

In 1637 Archbishop Laud and the 'Court of Star Chamber' sentenced three Puritans to have their ears cut off and their cheeks branded. They were also heavily fined and sent to prison. One of them, William Prynne, was a lawyer who had written against the bishops. He had been an MP in the 1620s and in 1640 he was elected MP again. In this 1640 cartoon, Laud and Prynne are on the left. Laud wears the big hat. Prynne is holding his ear-stumps.

C SOURCE

The House of Commons in 1624. The Speaker sits in the central chair. The clerks who kept the records sit at the table.

The Church and the Puritans

During the years 1603–40 the disagreement between the **bishops** and **archbishops** of the Church of England and the Puritans (see page 15) grew much worse. The Puritans were certain that they knew what God wanted, and that God had chosen them to lead others in the fight against sin. They preached sermons and printed pamphlets to spread their ideas. King Charles and Archbishop Laud believed just as firmly that God had appointed them to lead the Church; everybody else – clergy, nobles, gentry and ordinary people – must respect their authority. Laud did his best to ban Puritan books and to imprison Puritan writers and preachers.

The kings' money problems and Parliament

James and Charles were both lavish spenders. As prices went on rising, they were always short of money. In the years 1603–29 they often called a Parliament to ask for extra **taxes**. But the House of Commons always discussed any complaints **before** it voted taxes. MPs had no control over the king's policies, but they did expect the king to listen to their complaints and worries. So the Lords and MPs who disliked Buckingham complained about him in Parliament. The Puritan MPs complained about the Church. Parliaments often ended in a row between the king and the House of Commons. After an unusually bitter argument in 1629, Charles called no more Parliaments for the next eleven years.

Laud

Archbishop William Laud (1573–1645) was the youngest of a family of ten, and the only boy. He worked all the time and had few friends. He hated Puritans and had great respect for authority. He became a teacher at Oxford, and Charles I made him archbishop. He tried to stop Puritan books and preaching, which made him many enemies. He was also blamed for the Scots rebellion against the new Prayer Book. Parliament accused him of treason in 1640, and in 1641 he was tried and imprisoned in the Tower. The charge of treason was nonsense. He had worked for the king, not against. But men like William Prynne MP were eager for revenge. In 1645 he was executed.

Ship Money

James and Charles tried many other ways to get more money, as well as asking Parliament for extra taxes. For instance, James greatly increased the **customs duties** (taxes on imports and exports). The House of Commons objected, but the king went on collecting the money just the same. During the years 1629–40, when Charles called no Parliaments, his ministers had to find other ways to raise money. The most important was collecting **'Ship Money'** to pay for the navy.

The coastal counties had always paid Ship Money in wartime. But Charles collected it from all over the country in peacetime. From 1635 he made it into a regular tax. So it looked as if he had solved his problem. He might never have to call a Parliament again – as long as there were no expensive wars.

Was the king above the law?

These arguments – over taxes, over the Church, over the king's rights or Parliament's rights – usually came down in the end to an argument about the **law**. Everybody agreed that the law was the king's law; he appointed the judges and sacked them if he didn't like them. But most people also felt that the king should stick to the law too, except in very special emergencies. Clever tricks like collecting Ship Money seemed to stretch the law to make the king more powerful.

The king also used his council as a law court, where people like Laud and Strafford could fine or imprison people, or even have their ears cut off (but not their heads). The **Court of Star Chamber** (Source B) was this sort of court. There was no jury, and this made it easy for the king to get things done. But these courts seemed to place the king above the law.

Scotland

It was a **Scots rebellion** that forced Charles to call an English Parliament again in 1640. The bishops had little power in the Scottish Church. It was controlled by committees of clergy, nobles and gentry. Charles wanted to control it himself through the bishops. In 1637 he introduced a new form of service in Scotland, without consulting the committees. When the new services were held, there were riots in the churches. In 1638 the Scots drew up the **National Covenant**. This was a vow to defend their own Church against the king and the bishops. Everybody who mattered in Scotland signed it.

D SOURCE

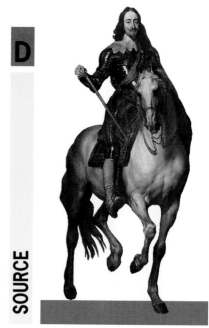

King Charles I, painted in 1633. Charles was a man of great dignity, but not a natural leader. He spoke badly was shy and reserved, and had no real friends among the English nobles after Buckingham's death.

John Hampden

John Hampden was a rich country gentleman. In the 1620s he was an MP. In 1636 he refused to pay his Ship Money, on the grounds that the king had no right to collect it. After a long trial, most of the judges came down on the king's side. Hampden had to pay. But some of the judges had said that Hampden was in the right. In 1641 he was a Member of the Parliament which made Ship Money illegal.

E SOURCE

It is blasphemy to dispute what God can do, or to say that a king cannot do this or that.

King James I in 1616.

Charles sent troops to force Scotland to obey him, but the Scots easily beat them. It would cost a great deal to raise a proper army, and Charles called Parliament to ask for extra taxes. Instead the MPs began to discuss their complaints about the events of the last eleven years. After three weeks Charles dissolved (dismissed) the Parliament. **Strafford** now patched together a makeshift army. But with no money and no public support, it had little chance. The Scots organized a much better army, collected money to pay for it and marched into England. The king was forced to sign a truce. He had to agree to pay the Scots £850 a day and let them occupy Newcastle-upon-Tyne. Only another Parliament could provide this sort of money. What would the MPs ask for before they voted it?

F SOURCE

Queen Henrietta Maria, wife of Charles I, painted in 1638. She was French, a devout Catholic and loved dancing and acting. Charles loved her, and often took her advice.

G SOURCE

A cartoon about the events of 1637 in Scotland, drawn at the time. 'Arch-Prelate' means archbishop.

Strafford

Thomas Wentworth (1593–1641), Earl of Strafford, ruled the North of England and Ireland for Charles I in the 1630s. He felt Britain needed a strong monarchy, and that people who opposed it should be firmly dealt with. People feared him but obeyed him. Charles I never liked him and only called him to London in 1639 when the Scots rebelled. Wentworth had been an MP, and felt the king should work with Parliament to solve the problem. He suggested calling one, but it was too late. England was seething with discontent. There was no money and no army to keep order or to fight the Scots. In 1640 Wentworth suggested that Charles should get control of the House of Commons by arresting the opposing MPs. The MPs heard of this and had Strafford arrested.

They put through an act declaring him guilty of treason. Charles had promised him protection, but Strafford feared the MPs would attack the queen next. He advised the king to sign the act. Charles did, but said later it was the worst thing he had ever done.

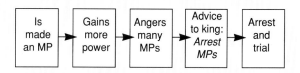

| Is made an MP | → | Gains more power | → | Angers many MPs | → | Advice to king: *Arrest MPs* | → | Arrest and trial |

Steps to Strafford's Fall

4.3 The Civil Wars

How the Civil Wars started

When **Parliament** met in November 1640 it had **Charles I** at its mercy. In October the king had agreed to pay the Scots £850 a day to stop their army marching south. He could only get money like this from Parliament. But during the eleven years without Parliament, Charles had annoyed most of the people who mattered. Above all, he had annoyed the English MPs. What would they demand before they would vote money to Charles?

John Pym was the MP who took the lead in the House of Commons. He accused Charles's two closest advisers, **Laud** and **Strafford**, of **high treason**, and had them arrested. Charles dared not order their release. When Pym saw that Strafford was likely to be found not guilty, he got Parliament to pass an Act which stated (without proof) that Strafford was a traitor. Charles signed, and in May 1641 Strafford was executed.

After that, other Acts of Parliament took away the king's power to rule without Parliament or to force people to obey his orders (see box). In August 1641 Charles signed all these laws, and the Scots army was paid off. So you might think that all the problems had been solved. From now on king and Parliament would have to work together.

John Pym and his friends weren't sure of this. They didn't trust Charles. They thought he would try to use force to get back all his power. Then, in October 1641 came dreadful news from **Ireland**. The Catholic Irish had rebelled and murdered many of the English Protestant settlers. Everybody was horrified. An army had to be sent as soon as possible to punish the rebels. But could the king be trusted with an army? Pym demanded that Parliament should appoint the general, not the king.

Some MPs thought this took too much power from the king. They began to build up a 'king's party' in Parliament. But Charles now made his worst mistake. He marched into the House of Commons with soldiers and tried to arrest Pym and four other MPs. How could the House trust him after that? Pym and his friends went into hiding, but they soon came out when the king left London. Charles set about raising an army. He intended to show the MPs who was master.

King Charles agreed in 1641 that:

- he would call a Parliament at least every three years.
- he would not dissolve the **present** Parliament without its own consent.
- he would give up his special law courts like the Star Chamber.
- no new taxes could be imposed without parliament's agreement.

Pym

John Pym (1584–1643) was a Puritan gentleman from Somerset who led the House of Commons in their attacks on Charles I's policies. Pym sat in every parliament during the years 1614–43, and knew exactly how to organize protest. He was expert at publicity. He used pamphlets and news-sheets to spread his views and kept the London crowds on his side.

Pym forced the king to give way over the fate of Strafford. He suggested reductions in royal power as shown above and forced Charles to accept them. No wonder Charles tried to arrest him in 1642. When the Second Civil War began, Pym organized raising Parliament's army and the taxes to pay it. He brought the Scots into the war on Parliament's side. Pym's death was a great loss for Parliament, as he was the one man who might have kept Parliament united and made a treaty with the king.

The First Civil War, 1642–6

The king's aim was to march to London and arrest the leading MPs. Parliament's aim was to stop him. There were many battles in 1642–4, but no knock-out blow. In 1643 Pym made a treaty with the Scots. In 1644 Parliament's army, with Scottish help, defeated a large Royalist army at **Marston Moor**. Then in 1645 Parliament raised a new army. This **New Model Army** smashed Charles's main army in its first battle at **Naseby** (1645). By 1646 Charles was a prisoner. What sort of peace would there be?

The Second Civil War, 1648

The king hoped to be able to get the army, the Scots and Parliament to fight each other. In the army many quite poor people had learned that they could fight as well as gentlemen (or better). Now they said that they should have a vote in elections for Parliament. Also, they believed that they should be able to worship God however they wished, not in a Church run by the richer people. This horrified most MPs and the Scots leaders.

So in 1648 the king, from his prison, was able to do a deal with the Scots, starting a new civil war. It didn't last long. The army marched north, smashed the Scots at **Preston** and crushed the English Royalists.

Why the New Model Army always won.

First rate training and discipline

Top quality weapons

Regular pay (except in 1647). The army cost about a million pounds a year

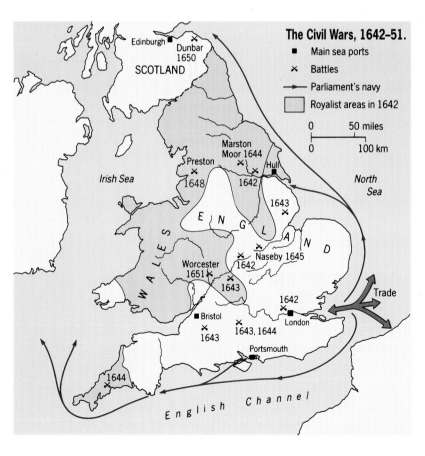

The Civil Wars, 1642–51.
- ■ Main sea ports
- ✕ Battles
- → Parliament's navy
- ▨ Royalist areas in 1642

The trial and execution of the king

One MP, Oliver Cromwell, had done more than anyone else to train the army and lead it to victory. He and his friends were now certain that they could never trust a king who had started two wars. As long as Charles lived there would be more Royalist rebellions. All the army's victories seemed clear proof of what God wanted. So, to make God's victory safe for the future, the army leaders decided to try the king and to execute him.

The existing law courts – the king's courts – could not try a king. Parliament would have to set up a special court. The army leaders knew that only 50 or 60 MPs would vote for this, so they sent troops (under **Colonel Pride**) to keep out more than 100 MPs and arrest those who objected. This was known as **Pride's Purge**. Then the **Rump** of the Commons, the MPs who were left, set up a court to try the king.

Charles behaved with great dignity, but the verdict was bound to go against him. In January 1649 he was executed in Whitehall. The Rump went on to pass laws to abolish the monarchy and the House of Lords and to give itself full power to rule and make laws. For the next four years these MPs ruled England.

Ireland and Scotland: more fighting, 1649–51

Charles I's son, **Charles Stuart**, now claimed that he was King Charles II, rightful ruler of all three kingdoms. The leaders of the Rump knew he would get plenty of support in Scotland and Ireland. So they sent Oliver Cromwell first to Ireland and then to Scotland to overthrow the Royalists there.

Nothing could stand in Cromwell's way. In Ireland he crushed the Royalists and the Irish Catholics. He sent the Scots flying at the Battle of **Dunbar** and took control of Edinburgh in 1650. Charles II still had enough support to raise a new army and march into England in 1651, but Cromwell cornered him at **Worcester** and destroyed his army. (Charles escaped in disguise.) Worcester was the last battle of the Civil Wars.

However often we beat him in battle, he is still God's anointed King.

Nine out of ten Englishmen are against the execution.

If God _wasn't_ on _our_ side, how did we come to win all the battles?

Charles Stuart is a man of blood. He started _both_ Civil Wars.

What if we cut off his head with the crown upon it!?

How could we ever trust him? If he had power, he'd execute _us_ as traitors!

Treason is fighting against the King. How can we execute _him_ for that?

He fought against the people and Parliament which is a lot worse!

Some arguments about what to do with Charles I in 1648–9.

SOURCE

A

The execution of Charles I in 1649.

Fairfax

Sir Thomas Fairfax (1612–71) was the son of Lord Fairfax, a Yorkshire landowner. When the First Civil War broke out he and his son Sir Thomas raised a Yorkshire army to fight for Parliament. Sir Thomas had fought in Holland and France, and had been planning to join the Swedish army when the First Civil War broke out. He understood soldiering. Both father and son took part in the Parliamentary victory of Marston Moor. When Parliament raised the New Model Army they chose Sir Thomas Fairfax to command it, because he was an experienced professional, and he was also not an MP. Under his command the army crushed the Royalists in both the civil wars.

When the wars were over and the king was put on trial, Fairfax couldn't decide what to do, so he did nothing. He would not sit as one of the judges, but made no attempt to save the king. His wife, Ann, went to the trial and shouted: 'Oliver Cromwell is a traitor!' Maybe he asked her to do this. A year later he resigned his command of the army, retired to his Yorkshire estates, and spent his time studying and writing books. When the Protectorate collapsed, he advised the army leaders to restore Charles II and elect a new parliament. He was elected MP for Yorkshire in 1660 and went to Holland to invite the new king back. Then he went back into retirement again until his death.

4.4 Britain Without a King

During the **Civil Wars** the old system of controlling people's opinions through the Church broke down. All sorts of people could say what they thought. They had plenty to argue about round army camp-fires, at prayer meetings or in alehouses. Should there be an organized Church or freedom of religion? What did God want, and why had He allowed the king to be defeated and executed? How should the country be ruled, now there was no king? Why shouldn't ordinary people have a say, as well as those who owned property?

Between 1640 and 1660 books and pamphlets flooded out of the printing presses asking questions like these and suggesting answers. For many who had fought against the king, it seemed a time of excitement and hope.

Not everyone felt like this. Many of the **gentry** and rich merchants who ran the villages and towns were worried. They thought people of low rank should be kept in their place. It was in the **army** that the excitement and hope were strongest, but even the army had no clear plans. Most of the generals, like Cromwell himself, were gentlemen and believed that power must be kept in the hands of the richer people. The only thing that the whole army agreed on was that everybody – except Catholics – should be allowed to worship God in their own way.

The Commonwealth, 1649–53

In 1649 the **Rump** made England into a **republic**, a country with no king or queen. The leaders of the Rump were in a very strong position. They had an unbeaten army and navy, and money to pay for both. This money came from new **taxes** that Parliament had agreed to during the Civil Wars, and from **fines** on the defeated Royalists. With the army the Rump could keep a firm grip on the country. It looked quite likely that the King of France or the King of Spain might send help to the Royalists, but the navy could put a stop to that.

A SOURCE

The front cover of a pamphlet called 'The World Turned Upside Down', published about 1647.

B SOURCE

Thus saith the Lord. As the Bishops, Charles and the Lords have had their turn, so shall your turn be next, ye surviving great ones, whoever you are that oppose me, the Eternal God.

From a pamphlet published in 1650.

C SOURCE

We have by our recent efforts shown how highly we value our just freedom. To avoid the danger of returning to a slavish condition, we declare that the people shall choose themselves a Parliament once every two years.

From a document published in 1647.

Ireland After the army and navy had seized complete control of Ireland and Scotland (page 40), the Rump kept troops permanently in both. In Ireland they confiscated the land of any Irish people who had fought against them (this meant most large landowners). Then they sold or gave the land to English Protestants, many of them soldiers from the army. Some Irish Catholics were moved to the west of Ireland, and others were sent to the West Indies. For the next 250 years most of the large landowners in Ireland were English Protestants, but the poor people who worked on their land were Irish Catholics.

War with the Dutch At this time the Dutch were by far the most important trading nation in Europe. Dutch ships carried the goods of all countries, including the English colonies, in and out of Britain. In 1651 the Rump passed a law forbidding this. From now on, foreigners could only trade in their own goods, and the English Empire was closed to foreign traders. This caused a war in 1652–4. The English fleet cut off Dutch trade almost entirely and won most of the battles.

Cromwell expels the Rump The MPs in the Rump did nothing to satisfy any of the high hopes for a better England. They just ran the country through a council made up of their own leaders. In 1653 it looked as if they planned to make this into a permanent system. Cromwell and the army lost patience, and turned out the MPs by force.

I do not find anything in the law of God that a Lord should choose 20 MPs, a gentleman two and a poor man none. The poorest he that is in England has a right to live as much as the greatest he.

From a speech made in 1647.

We plough and dig so that the poor may get a living. We have right to it because of the conquest over the late King. Parliament said: 'Risk your lives with us and we will make you free people.' Therefore we claim the freedom to enjoy common lands bought by our money and blood.

From a pamphlet published in 1650.

I think that no man has a right to share in the affairs of the Kingdom if he owns no property in the Kingdom.

From a speech made in 1647.

Lilburne

John Lilburne (1614?–1657) was a London clothworker, who fought for Parliament in the First Civil War, but refused to join the New Model Army, and did not fight again. He believed that people had the right to freedom of speech and religion. For saying and printing what he thought he was either sent to prison or exiled by every government from 1637–54. Many people agreed with what he said in his pamphlets, and formed a group called the Levellers. They wanted all men to have a vote, and, through Parliament, to have complete control of the country.

Lilburne was popular with the ordinary people of London; London juries usually acquitted him. Rich gentry and wealthy merchants said he was a hot-head, as did Cromwell and other army leaders. He encouraged the ordinary soldiers to insist on their rights and to refuse to obey orders. His opponents found it impossible to shut him up – he went on arguing his case in pamphlets written in prison and published. It was a long time before his ideas were accepted.

The Protectorate, 1653–9

The army leaders tried for six years to find a new system that could satisfy some of the high hopes for a better England. They called several Parliaments, with MPs from Ireland and Scotland as well as from England and Wales. They made **Cromwell** ruler for life, with the title of **Protector** instead of King.

Cromwell had a magic quality of leadership. People – even many Royalists – trusted and admired him. Above all, people knew how successful he was; a not very important country gentleman had become ruler of a powerful nation! People thought this must be the work of God. Cromwell tried hard to work with his Parliaments. He was himself a landowner and a former MP, and he wanted to put back much of the old system though without a king at the top. But he could never get a Parliament to agree.

War with Spain England had a powerful army and navy which had won the Civil Wars and taken complete control over the British Isles. As a result, some people felt certain that God meant Englishmen to do great things in Europe and the world. Cromwell decided that an English navy should sail to **America** to overthrow the Spanish Empire. So in 1655 he sent a fleet to attack the Spanish West Indies. It wasn't very successful, but it did capture the island of Jamaica. More important was the use of the fleet to cut off the supply of American silver on which Spain depended. This meant that the King of Spain couldn't pay his armies. Then Cromwell sent troops across the Channel to help the French who were at war with Spain. In 1659 (after Cromwell's death) Spain accepted defeat, leaving England in control of the port of Dunkirk in the Spanish Netherlands and of Jamaica.

The end of the Protectorate Although Cromwell was successful abroad, the wars interfered with peaceful trade and cost a lot of money. He died in September 1658, and for a short time his son Richard ruled as Protector. But in 1659 Richard resigned. Now the army had no clear leader. All the attempts to rule without a king seemed to have failed. Even with the extra taxes, money was running out, and there wasn't enough to pay the army. What might this lead to?

G SOURCE

A painting of Cromwell, from about 1650. He said: 'Paint my picture truly like me, pimples, warts and all, as you see me.'

H SOURCE

Keep out, you cynic not here.

Sir, I bring good cheere.

Old C welco not h

A cartoon from 1653 – the figure in the middle is Father Christmas. The Rump passed a law to ban Christmas feasts and parties.

I SOURCE

His Highness the Lord Protector of the Commonwealth of England, Scotland and Ireland and the dominions thereto belonging.

Oliver Cromwell's full title as Lord Protector, 1653–8.

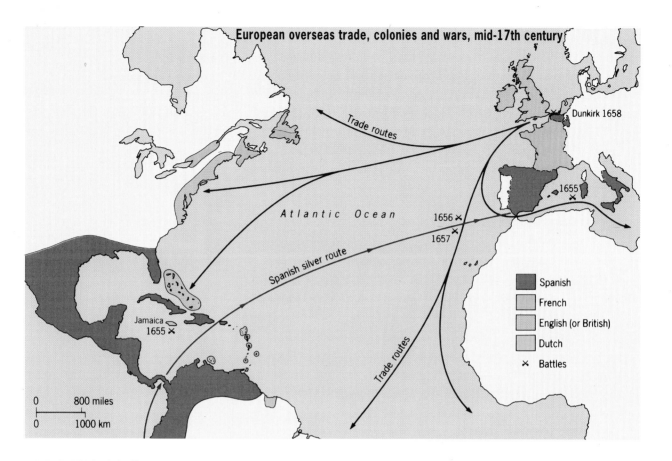

European overseas trade, colonies and wars, mid-17th century

Trade routes

Dunkirk 1658

Atlantic Ocean

Spanish silver route

1655

1656 ×
1657 ×

Jamaica
1655 ×

Trade routes

Spanish
French
English (or British)
Dutch
× Battles

0   800 miles
0   1000 km

Cromwell

Oliver Cromwell (1599–1658) inherited his father's small estate and married a London merchant's daughter in 1620. They had four sons and four daughters. Cromwell was a convinced Puritan with a burning sense of duty to carry out God's will. Cromwell took only a small part in politics until the Civil Wars began. Then he organized and led his own regiment of cavalry – the 'Ironsides'. In 1645 he helped to organize the New Model Army. The main idea behind this new army was that it should be made up of soldiers and officers who believed they were fighting God's battles. He also insisted on strict discipline and drill, and top quality weapons. Cromwell himself turned out to be a great leader on the battlefield and a genius in organizing the armies. It was a deadly combination – he never lost a battle.

Cromwell and his friends were sure that their victory in the Civil Wars was part of God's purpose, and that God intended a glorious future for all Englishmen afterwards. Instead there were rebellions, disagreements and disappointment. As an MP, Cromwell believed the country should be run by an elected Parliament. He also believed in religious freedom. He was certain that to put the king back on the throne was against God's will, and would lead to religious persecution. He refused the suggestion that he should be made king himself, but agreed to become 'Protector'. He tried hard to get support from the landowners and rich merchants, but died before he had got very far. He was buried in Westminster Abbey. After the Restoration his body was dug up and hanged in public.

Back to normal

In 1660 most people could see that the attempt to rule without a king had failed. Parliament invited **Charles II** to come home and take over. Charles was very intelligent, and he knew that he could only rule successfully by working with the nobles and gentry in Parliament. So he accepted the **limits on the king's power** that his father had agreed to in 1641. Parliament restored the **Church of England** too, and dismissed the Puritan clergy from their jobs.

London survives plague and fire

Charles II's reign was a time of prosperity. Trade improved, and people were contented. England quickly recovered from disasters like the **Great Plague** (1665) and the **Fire of London** (1666). The plague probably killed up to 100,000 Londoners, and the fire burned down most of central London – the houses there were still mostly made of wood. But once the fire died out, Londoners began to rebuild. They kept most of the old narrow streets, but they built their new houses of brick, so there were no more widespread fires. London was soon bigger than ever.

A problem for the future

Charles secretly preferred the Catholic religion, but he kept quiet about this until he was on his death-bed. His brother **James** was less intelligent and more honest; he was a devout Catholic, and made no secret of it. Charles had no legitimate children (he had plenty of illegitimate ones), so it became clear that James would be the next king. How could a Catholic be king of Protestant Britain?

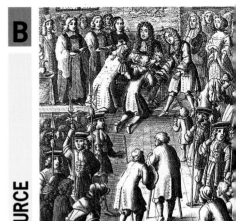

B SOURCE

Charles II touching sick people for the 'king's evil' – scrofula. A drawing made in 1684. Kings of England were said to be able to cure sufferers from the disease by just touching them.

Laws against Puritans
- Only Church of England services allowed.
- Puritan schoolmasters and clergy sacked.
- Those sacked had to move at least five miles from where they had worked.

Many Puritans still refused to conform to the Church. They became known as **Nonconformists**.

The Fire of London, September 1666, painted soon afterwards.

A SOURCE

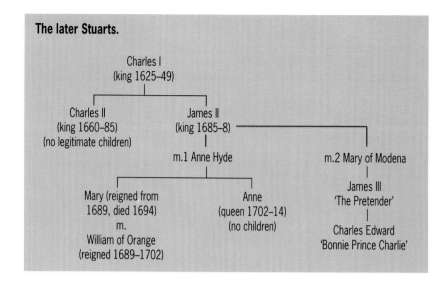

The later Stuarts.

```
                    Charles I
                  (king 1625–49)
          ┌────────────────┴────────────────┐
      Charles II                        James II
    (king 1660–85)                   (king 1685–8) ──────────────────┐
 (no legitimate children)               │                            │
                                   m.1 Anne Hyde              m.2 Mary of Modena
                          ┌─────────────┴─────────────┐              │
                   Mary (reigned from            Anne            James III
                    1689, died 1694)        (queen 1702–14)    'The Pretender'
                          m.                  (no children)          │
                  William of Orange                           Charles Edward
                   (reigned 1689–1702)                      'Bonnie Prince Charlie'
```

SOURCE

C

The Lieutenant of the Tower tells me that the fire began this morning in the King's baker's house in Pudding Lane. In an hour's time the fire ranged every way – the wind mighty high and driving it into the city, and everything after so long a drought proving burnable.

From Samuel Pepys's Diary, 2 September 1666.

D

People think that there has been some kind of plot in this (the fire). Many have been arrested. It has been dangerous for any stranger to walk in the street.

From Pepys's Diary, 6 September 1666.

E

I have been this afternoon in the committee examining persons suspected of firing the City. But people are generally satisfied that the fire was accidental.

A letter from Sir T. Osborne MP, 2 October 1666.

F

The Frenchman who was said to fire the City and was hanged for it, confessed that he did – with a stick – reach in a fireball at a window of the king's baker.

From Pepys's Diary, 24 February 1667. The Frenchman was Robert Hubert, a watchmaker. He said that he was a Catholic. He was hanged on 27 October 1666.

Pepys

Samuel Pepys (1633–1703) was the son of a tailor. Pepys was given a good education but he inherited no money. When he was 22 years old he took a job as secretary to a rich cousin and married a French girl who was only 15 years old. The cousin became an admiral, and Pepys worked in the Navy Office in London from 1659 until he retired in 1689. His efficient organization played an important part in providing Britain with a navy which could claim to be the best in the world.

For nine years, from 1660–69, Pepys kept a diary. He wrote in code, so that he could keep secret details about the people he met, about his own personal thoughts, and about his many girlfriends. He often went to court and knew Charles II and James II and all the leading people of the time. He had a sharp eye and a lively pen, so his diary is both interesting and important. He had no children and left all his books including the diary to his old college. Pepys's secret code was not cracked until 1825. Historians have been using his diary with delight ever since.

James II's reign, 1685–88

James II took over with very little trouble. Nobody wanted another civil war. Most people had great respect for the Crown, and James was popular even if he was a Catholic. People knew that he had no sons, and his daughters Mary and Anne were both determined Protestants. James, aged 54, was quite old by 17th-century standards. The next British rulers after he died would be Mary and her husband William. William of Orange, as he was called, was leader of the Dutch nation. He was a hero to all Protestants because of his successful fight against Catholic France. It looked as if God had arranged things just right for the Protestants!

James moved fast. He strengthened the army and began to appoint Catholics as officers. He asked Parliament to change the laws so as to allow Catholics to be army officers and government ministers. When Parliament refused, he dissolved it and simply declared that the laws no longer applied. He announced that everybody, including Catholics and Nonconformists, could worship as they liked. He sacked judges whom he didn't trust, and stopped all the gentry who were against these changes from being JPs. (This meant most of the gentry.) The Archbishop of Canterbury and six other bishops protested about the changes, so James had them arrested.

The Revolution of 1688

Just at this tense moment, Queen Mary gave birth to a son. This made things quite different. It meant that Britain might have Catholic rulers for a long time. Seven leading nobles decided that they had to act now or never. They wrote to William of Orange in Holland and asked him to bring a Dutch army to England, promising to help him if he did.

A playing card of 1689, showing how the baby might have been secretly smuggled in.

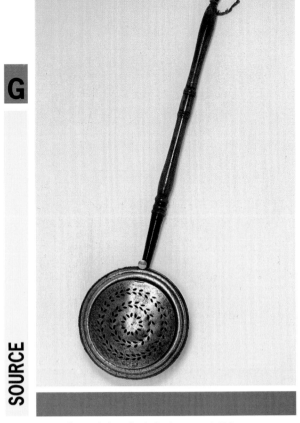

Protestants claimed that the baby born in 1688 was not really James II's son, but had been smuggled into the queen's bed in a warming pan like this one. Warming pans, containing hot coals, were used to warm the bed.

The Queen is brought to bed of a Boy

Reported fo

William landed in October 1688 and James's support quickly melted away. His best troops went over to William's side, while he himself fled to France. Elections were held for a new Parliament. In 1689 Parliament passed laws saying that William and Mary were now rulers instead of James.

Over the next few years other laws (see box) made it clear that the king or queen could never hope to rule without the support of Parliament. No ruler since James II has tried. The British system has been a partnership between king or queen and Parliament ever since, with Parliament becoming gradually more and more powerful.

Religion: a little bit of freedom

James II had stopped the persecution of Nonconformists to try to get them on his side. But most of them had refused, and they supported William in 1688. Some MPs wanted to reward them by allowing religious freedom, but many of the country gentry opposed this. In 1689 Nonconformists were allowed to have their own religious services. But they were still not allowed to be MPs, hold any government job, or even go to university. The persecution of Nonconformists and of Catholics came to an end. But they remained second-class citizens of the country for another 150 years.

Margaret Fell

Margaret Fell (1614–1702) married Thomas Fell, a lawyer from northern Lancashire, when she was 18 years old. They had nine children. Thomas became a judge, and was often away, so Margaret often ran the household. She brought up the children and ran a large estate which included an iron works. In 1652 George Fox, the founder of the Quakers, persuaded her to join his new religious group, the Society of Friends. Quakers refused to go to church or pay towards it, but held meetings in each others' houses. Fox argued that nobody had a special right to tell other people what God wanted. They refused to swear oaths, and would not show special respect to anyone, even the king, by bowing or taking off their hats.

Thomas Fell did not join the Society, but he let Margaret hold meetings at their house, which became a centre for the spread of Quakerism in the north. Thomas died in 1658 and in 1669 Margaret married George Fox. She and George were often arrested and sent to prison for breaking the laws against Puritans. On two occasions she got George out of prison by going to see the king in person. They collected money to help others in trouble, and helped to set up and run a network of local and countrywide meetings. They even set up meetings in the American colonies. The Society of Friends is active worldwide today. Margaret and George lived long enough to gain religious freedom in 1689.

Britain Takes a Lead in Science

The new science

Before 1500 **scientific knowledge** was based on the ideas of the Ancient Greeks. If you saw something with your own eyes that didn't seem to fit the Greek ideas, you assumed you were wrong, not the Greeks. But in the 16th century, people began to think that the Greeks could be wrong. For instance, the 16th-century Polish astronomer **Copernicus** showed that the Greeks were probably wrong to think that the Sun went round the Earth. By 1650 other astronomers in Italy and Germany had measured the movement of the planets with great accuracy, and proved that Copernicus was right. Science since that time has been based not on ancient books but on careful observation and measurement of what we can see for ourselves.

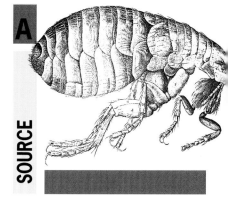

A

SOURCE

A flea drawn by Robert Hooke using an early microscope in 1665. Hooke worked for the Royal Society.

The first important British scientist was **William Harvey**, a London doctor. In 1628 Harvey showed that the Greeks were wrong about the movement of the blood in the human body. He proved that his own theory of the **circulation of the blood** was right by exact measurements. Everyone who repeated his experiments could see that he was right. It was a long time before Harvey's work helped doctors to cure sick people, but straight away it showed scientists that this new 'experimental' science was the real way forward.

Before Copernicus

The Sun goes round the Earth in a circle every day. So do the planets and the Moon.

I agree, because it fits in with what the Bible says in Joshua, Chapter 10, verse 13.

Yes. The circle is a perfect shape - so the Sun is **bound** to move in a circle.

Me too. It fits in with all the famous Greek writers.

After Newton

The Earth goes around the Sun once a year. Its orbit is **not** a circle.

It's the force of gravity that pulls the Earth and the Sun together.

Yes - It's the same force that pulls this apple down off the tree. Isaac Newton has measured it exactly.

Every time I check the measurements I get the same as Newton! His calculations are dead right too. You can't disagree.

After the Civil Wars the new science became popular among learned and fashionable people in England. In 1660 a group of them, supported by King Charles II, formed the **Royal Society** in London. The Society ran experiments, published the work of British scientists and exchanged ideas with foreign ones. Its members made much improved scientific instruments like microscopes and telescopes, and really accurate clocks. They did a great deal to lay the foundations of modern physics, chemistry and the other sciences.

The greatest Royal Society member by far was **Sir Isaac Newton**. He put together the ideas of all the astronomers since Copernicus into one complete theory of the working of the solar system. Using the improved telescopes and new types of mathematics that he had developed himself, he worked out the exact strength of the **force of gravity**. In 1687 he showed how it held the solar system together. Newton was able to predict the movements of the planets and the Moon in their orbits, or of an apple falling from a tree. His calculations proved exactly right – 20th-century space satellites still use them. Newton's work was an enormous triumph for the new science, and placed Britain firmly among its leaders.

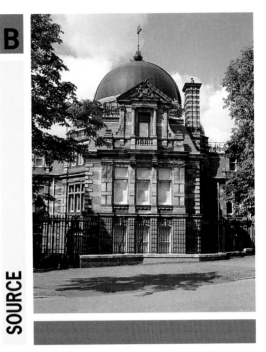

B SOURCE

Greenwich Royal Observatory, built in 1676. King Charles II appointed an Astronomer Royal to work out the exact position of Greenwich, and of various stars as seen from there. Sailors anywhere in the world could observe the same stars and work out their position compared with that of Greenwich. The Greenwich Meridian is still the base-line for world maps.

Newton

Sir Isaac Newton (1642–1727) lived with his grandmother when he was very young. His father had died before he was born and his mother had re-married. Newton went to the local Grammar School in Lincolnshire. When he was 14 years old he left school to help his uncle run the family farm. Newton was always reading, calculating and working out how things worked. His uncle said he should go to Cambridge University instead.

He was 19 years old when he went there in 1661. By 1669 he was a professor. He made many of his most brilliant discoveries from 1664–67, though it took him years to work out the details, and prove that his theories fitted the facts.

He was lucky that many discoveries in science and maths had been made earlier in the century – he said later, 'I have stood upon the shoulders of giants'. However, it was his insight and skill that put all the discoveries together. In 1687 he published a book which explained the new science. Newton was a Fellow, and later the President, of the Royal Society. He was MP for Cambridge for many years. He was Master of the Mint and helped to organize a new coinage. He also studied the Bible, writing books about what it foretold. On his death he was buried in Westminster Abbey, showing how important science had become in Britain.

5.1 Ireland and Scotland

In 1689 the English overthrew James II and put William and Mary on the English throne without bloodshed. It was very different in Ireland and Scotland.

Ireland

Under a Catholic king, James II, things were better for the Irish Catholics. James let them worship freely, and sit as MPs in the Irish Parliament. By 1688 he had a large Catholic army in Ireland led by a Catholic general. When James fled from England his Irish supporters easily got control of most of the country. In 1689 James arrived there himself with a French army lent by his friend King Louis XIV. He called a Parliament in Dublin and it quickly passed laws taking back most of the land from the English and Scots settlers.

The only parts of Ireland not under James's control were those areas in **Ulster** where most people were British settlers. These Ulster Protestants slammed shut the gates of their walled city, **Londonderry**, in the face of James's troops. Their motto was 'No surrender!'. James's army cut off all food to the city, so without help from England the Protestants stood no chance. William could see the danger of letting James and the French get control of Ireland. In 1689 he sent warships to take food to Londonderry, and in 1690 he went to Ireland himself with a large army. The future of Ireland was settled at the Battle of the Boyne on 12 July 1690. James lost and fled to France.

Walker

George Walker (1618–90) was the son of an English settler in Ulster. He joined the church, and became a clergyman near Derry. In 1688–89 he raised a regiment of soldiers among the Protestant settlers to fight against James II. In 1689 James advanced on Derry, and Walker went to meet him. Walker persuaded the Governor of Derry to escape, and took over himself. James besieged Derry.

During the siege Walker helped to organize the food – they even ate rats. He also led attacks on James's troops. After 101 days the city was relieved. Walker went to London and was made a bishop as a reward. He was killed at the Battle of the Boyne.

A

A wall painting in Londonderry, from the 1980s. The picture on the left shows William at the Battle of the Boyne.

SOURCE

The Protestants in control The English and Scots Protestant settlers were now back in firm control. In most parts of Ireland they were outnumbered by far by Catholic Irish people. So they brought in more laws against Catholics. The aim was to destroy the leaders of the Irish, the gentry and educated people. On the whole this succeeded. Some Catholic gentry fled to France. Others sank into poverty. A few turned Protestant. Soon Protestants owned nearly all the land. The poorer Irish people worked as labourers or paid rent to their new landlords and rulers. But they spoke their own language and clung to their own religion and way of life.

> **Laws against Irish Catholics**
> A Catholic could not
> * vote or be an MP
> * go to university
> * be a lawyer
> * hold any government job
> * be a teacher
> * be a soldier
> * buy land from a Protestant
> * own a horse worth over £5.

Scotland

Most people in the **lowlands** of Scotland were determined Protestants. So in 1689 a Scots Parliament turned James off the throne and accepted William and Mary as rulers of Scotland.

But most Scottish highlanders were loyal to James. Many of them were Catholic. The highland clans often raided the lowlands to steal cattle, and they were used to fighting. The lowlanders looked on them as savages. In 1689 William's troops, with help from the lowlanders, defeated the highland army, and the clans then accepted William as king.

In spite of this, very few Scots people really believed that William was the rightful King of Scotland. He had been made king by Parliament and not by God. Many, especially in the highlands, longed for James to rule again. They became known as **Jacobites** (from 'Jacobus', the Latin form of the name James).

Events in Ireland and Scotland, 1688–90.

5.2 A Partly United Kingdom

In 1707 the Scots agreed to abolish their own Parliament, and instead to send Scots lords and MPs to a **'United Kingdom' Parliament** at Westminster. They still do. Why did the English want this, and why did the Scots agree? Both were proud nations. The two countries had been ruled by the same kings or queens since 1603, but English and Scots people still looked on each other as foreigners.

Danger – highlanders! Most members of Scotland's Parliament were lowlanders. They disliked the clansmen of the highlands far more than they disliked the English. So they were quite glad to have English troops in Scotland.

Danger – Jacobites! William and Mary had no children, and neither did **Queen Anne**. So **James Stuart**, the Catholic son of James II, had a strong claim to be the next king of Great Britain. There were plenty of Jacobites in England and Scotland who looked on him as 'James III'. (He was known as 'The Pretender' by non-Jacobites.) In 1701 the English Parliament chose **George of Hanover**, a Protestant, as their next king. What if the Scots chose James? Obviously this would lead to war between the two countries. France was already at war with Great Britain, and would probably send an army. So Britain would become a battleground again. Nobody wanted that.

Trade and wealth England was far richer than Scotland. The traders of the Scottish lowlands wanted a chance to share in this wealth and in England's growing overseas empire.

Flora Macdonald

Flora Macdonald (1722–90) was an orphan brought up by rich relatives on the Island of Skye. She attended an Edinburgh boarding school. In 1745 Prince Charles, who was on the run after Culloden, fled to an island where Flora was staying. She agreed to help him to escape, and dressed him up as her Irish maid. They went by rowing boat to Skye, where her relations (all Jacobites) lived. Here she hid the Prince in a cave and went to their castle. An officer working for King George was there but she secretly told her relations where Charles was, and they sent servants to help him to escape to France.

Flora was arrested, and taken prisoner to London, but later pardoned. She married a cousin and emigrated to America, but later came back to Scotland. She had eight children and lived happily until 1790.

A

SOURCE

The Battle of Culloden, painted in 1746. Captured clansmen posed for the artist.

The Jacobite rebellions

George I and George II were foreigners who usually spoke German or French. Few people really liked them. So there were many **Jacobite plots** and two serious **rebellions**, in 1715 and 1745. Both rebellions failed, mainly because the Pretender held firmly to his Catholic faith.

The '45, led by the Pretender's son, **Bonnie Prince Charlie**, was the most nearly successful. He was dashing, handsome and brave. At the head of an army of 5,000 highland clansmen, he won the first battle and got control of much of Scotland. Then he had to choose. He could either stay in Scotland and organize more support there, or he could march boldy south towards London. His most experienced advisers wanted to stay, but Charles believed that the magic of his name would bring the English nobles and gentry to his side. He led his highlanders as far as Derby, only 138 miles fom London. But no English people of any importance joined Charles. He still wanted to push on, but his officers persuaded him to march back to Scotland.

A cartoon published in London in 1745 with the title 'The Highland Visitors'.

By this time the king's son, the **Duke of Cumberland**, had an army ready. He cornered the Jacobites at **Culloden** near Inverness. Charles ordered his tired highlanders to charge uphill against twice their own number. Cumberland's men shot them to pieces. About half the highlanders were killed or captured. Many of the others were hunted down afterwards and slaughtered without mercy – Cumberland became known as 'Butcher'. Loyal highlanders helped Charles to escape to France. Culloden was the last battle fought on British soil.

The clans destroyed

After the '15 more forts were built in the highlands with roads to link them up. After the '45 the government set out to smash the clans completely. Laws were passed to destroy the power of the clan chiefs. The clansmen had to give up their weapons, and even their tartan kilts. Schools were set up, teaching in English only. Within 20 or 30 years the clan system was just a romantic memory. So was the claim of the Stuarts to be rightful kings, or of Scotland to be independent of England.

> **The Act of Union, 1707**
>
> **The Scots agreed that:**
> - in future there would be only one 'United Kingdom' Parliament. Scotland would send lords and MPs to sit at Westminster
> - George of Hanover was to be king of the whole United Kingdom when Anne died.
>
> **The English agreed that:**
> - Scots people had the same right to trade in any part of Britain or the Empire as English people
> - the Scots were to keep control of their own Church and their own law courts.

5.3 Why did Britain Gain an Empire?

In 1603 Britain had no **overseas colonies**, except Ireland. But by 1750 there was a British Empire in North America and the West Indies, with over a million colonists as well as large numbers of slaves. Other European countries had empires too. Europeans with their ships and guns could go anywhere and defeat anybody. But the **British Empire** was well on the way to becoming the richest and most powerful in the world. Why?

Trading companies

It cost a lot of money to start a new colony. You needed ships with enough guns to deal with any possible attack. You needed enough food and clothing to last the settlers for up to a year. You needed farming and building tools. And it could be years before you could bring anything back to Europe to sell to pay for all the expense. Even the richest London merchants could not afford this alone. So several of them put their money together. They shared the risk of their ships being lost in storms or the settlers being killed, and they shared any profit. **Trading companies** like this began most of the new colonies.

London was the best place to start a trading company. It had many rich merchants ready to take a risk with their money. Some of these companies failed, but the successful ones set up colonies in the West Indies and North America, and trading centres in India. They made high profits for the shareholders by selling tea from India and coffee, sugar and tobacco from America and the West Indies to all parts of Europe.

Who went to the colonies?

About 350,000 people went from Britain to settle in the new colonies during the 17th century. Some went for an exciting adventure. Many went for religious reasons. In the years 1620–40 many **Puritans** (see page 35) went to find a land where they could worship freely. The Puritans called the part of North America where they settled **New England**.

Most of those who went were poor people, hoping for land or work. (There were many poor people in 17th-century Britain: see page 24.) The trading companies let you travel free if you agreed to work as a labourer for seven years without pay – if you lived that long. Of 144 people who sailed to Virginia in 1607, 41 died on the way and 63 others died in their first year there.

SOURCE A

The coat of arms and the crest of John Hawkins. Hawkins made his fortune as a slave trader.

SOURCE B

They had no friends to welcome them, no houses. It was winter, and the winters of that country are sharp and hard. What could they see but a desolate wilderness, full of wild beasts and wild men? If they looked behind them there was the mighty ocean as a gulf to separate them from all the civilized parts of the world.

William Bradford, one of the leaders of the Puritan settlers in America, writing in 1645 about what it was like in 1620.

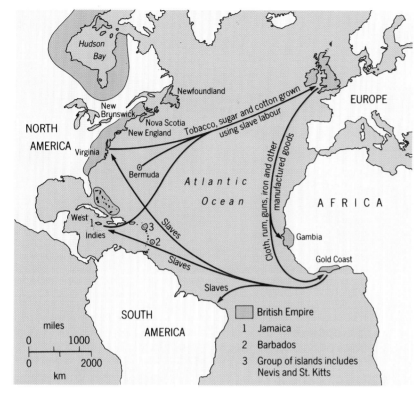

The 'triangular trade': the same ships could make a good profit on each 'leg' of the triangle.

Some colonies gained by government action:

1655 Cromwell captured **Jamaica**.
1660 Charles II married a Portuguese princess, and was given the Indian city of **Bombay** as a wedding present.
1664 **New York** was captured from the Dutch.
1704 **Gibraltar** was captured from Spain.
1688–1713 Wars with France. Britain gained **Newfoundland**, **Nova Scotia** and **Hudson's Bay**.

Slavery

The 'planters' growing sugar or tobacco in America and the West Indies soon found that **slaves** from Africa were cheaper than white labourers. Black people were believed to work better than whites in the tropical sun. As slaves they were paid nothing.

Government action

From about 1650 the British government began to use the navy to protect the new colonial trade and to keep foreigners out of it. It could see that the colonies were bringing in an excellent profit and helping to make Britain rich. From then on most of Britain's many wars were partly about the Empire and its trade.

SOURCE C

Owned by James Stone	Value
Thomas Groves, 4 years to serve	1,300 pounds of tobacco
Susan Davis, 3 years to serve	1,000 pounds of tobacco
Emaniel, a Negro man	2,000 pounds of tobacco
Mingo, a Negro man	2,000 pounds of tobacco

From a list of the property of James Stone, a Virginia planter, 1648.

Pocohantas

Pocohantas (1595–1617) was the daughter of an American Indian king with whom some of the Virginia settlers were friendly. John Smith, one of the settlers, was captured by the Indians. He claimed later that she had begged her father to spare him and so had saved his life. Although Smith probably made up this romantic story, Pocohantas did become friendly with the settlers.

John Rolfe was another settler. His wife and baby daughter had just died. In 1613 Pocohantas, then 16 years old, became a Christian and married Rolfe. She called herself Rebecca. They came to England in 1616, and Pocohantas caused great interest. She was received by the queen. But as they were getting ready to go back to Virginia in 1617 she died. They had no children. Rolfe went back to Virginia alone, and later married again.

5.4 Britain's Growing Wealth

The 100 years from 1650 to 1750 were a time of growing wealth for Britain. This was mainly because of **trade**. In 1750 British merchants could trade freely with the 14 million people in the British Empire. This gave them a big advantage over foreign merchants. But Britain was also the leading country in worldwide trade, with more ships than any other nation. **London** was the largest city in Europe and one of the richest in the world.

Industry was increasing too. Some industries were new, like sugar refining (purifying). But the old industry of making woollen cloth was much more important, and was richer than ever. Another old industry which grew rapidly was **coal mining**. Britain was really the only important coal-mining country in the world. It exported a million tonnes a year to the Continent. In Britain people used coal in brickworks, glassworks and saltworks, and these industries were able to grow fast too.

Farming In 1750 eight out of ten people still lived by farming. But many of them used new methods. This meant that they grew far more corn than before – enough to feed Britain and sell some to foreign countries. New crops, like turnips, meant that they could keep more cattle. As a result, food was cheap in Britain.

Trade, industry and prosperity in the British Isles, 1650–1750.

Liverpool
Imports from the colonies, including cotton. Liverpool merchants active in the slave trade

Northern Ireland
New linen industry set up by French protestant settlers

Shropshire
New iron-working area. 1710: Abraham Darby invented a way to use coal instead of wood in the furnace to make cast iron

Bristol
Imports and refines sugar and tobacco from the colonies

Dublin ●

Cornwall
1711: the first successful steam engine made by Thomas Newcomen to pump water out of the mines

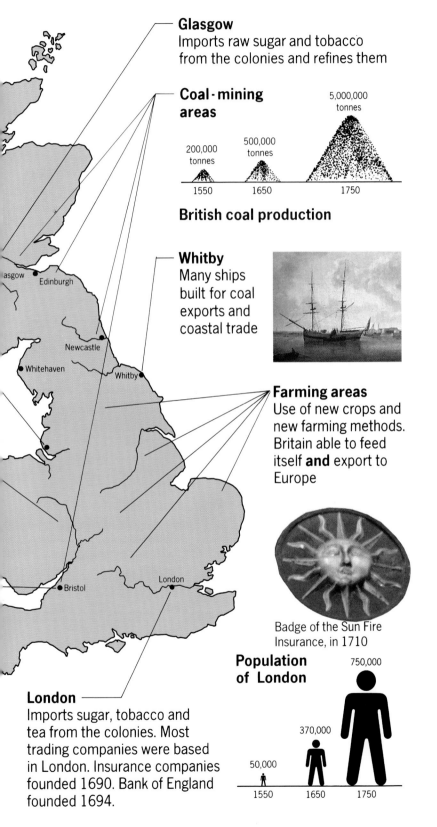

Glasgow
Imports raw sugar and tobacco from the colonies and refines them

Coal-mining areas

British coal production

5,000,000 tonnes

500,000 tonnes

200,000 tonnes

1550   1650   1750

Whitby
Many ships built for coal exports and coastal trade

Farming areas
Use of new crops and new farming methods. Britain able to feed itself **and** export to Europe

Badge of the Sun Fire Insurance, in 1710

Glasgow
Edinburgh
Newcastle
Whitehaven
Whitby
Bristol
London

London
Imports sugar, tobacco and tea from the colonies. Most trading companies were based in London. Insurance companies founded 1690. Bank of England founded 1694.

Population of London

750,000

370,000

50,000

1550   1650   1750

Without good **transport** these changes could not have happened. The roads were just mud tracks, which got steadily worse. But the rich farming and industrial areas were all near rivers or the sea coast. So it was easy to carry goods to and from most parts of Britain by boat.

The **City of London** was like a spider at the centre of a web of British trade. The **Bank of England** (founded in 1694) and other new **banks** made it easy for merchants and others to borrow and pay money. People could buy and sell shares in the trading companies from **stockbrokers**. **Insurance companies** would pay for the loss if a merchant's ship was sunk or his house burned down.

Lloyd

Edward Lloyd (?–1726?) ran a coffee house in London in the 1680s. No one is sure when he was born, or when he died.

Merchants and ship-owners met at his coffee house to bargain. London became a centre of worldwide trade. Lloyd's became the best place to find out about ships or arrange insurance. Later, the merchants meeting there formed a society, 'Lloyd's of London'. It still runs insurance and provides information about the world's ships.

5.5 Rich and Poor in 18th-Century Britain

SOURCE **A**

A country gentleman and family: Robert Gwillym of Atherton in Warwickshire in 1750.

For a **rich family** in 18th-century Britain, fashion was very important – fashionable houses, clothes and lifestyles. You could only get the 'right' jobs for your sons if you knew the 'right' people. It was important for sons and daughters to marry into families that might bring more land, wealth or honour to their families. So the **country houses** of rich people were large and impressive. There was room for many visitors with their servants and horses. There were large rooms for parties, dances and concerts. There was space to show off the paintings and statues that gentlemen brought back from their travels in Italy and France.

Fashionable families would spend part of the year in London, being seen at court and paying visits to friends. So they had to buy or rent a **London house** too. It was also fashionable to spend a few weeks at Bath, or one of the other **spas**. Here people could drink the medicinal waters for their health, show off their expensive clothes and hope to arrange good marriages for their children.

SOURCE **B**

Here I came to villages of sad little huts made up of only stones piled together and the roofs of slate. There seemed to be no tunnels for chimneys and no mortar or plaster. I took them at first sight for a sort of barns to feed cattle in, not thinking them to be dwelling houses.

From Celia Fiennes, 'Journeys', 1697. This extract describes the houses of the poor in Westmorland. Celia Fiennes was a rich gentlewoman from the south of England.

SOURCE

The London crowd at a public execution – a drawing by William Hogarth (1697–1764).

Conditions for many of the **poorer people** in England improved too. Many richer farmers and yeomen built comfortable new houses. Prices fell, so a person's wage would buy about twice as much in 1730 as in 1630. When people went to France, or to Ireland or Scotland, they often noticed that the poor people were worse fed, clothed and housed there than in England.

But for the **poorest people** of all, life was still very hard, especially in years of bad trade or poor harvest. The **Poor Law** meant that people could get help in their own village, but nowhere else. The London poor lived in crowded **slums**. Life there was unhealthy and often short.

SOURCE

We saw a small opening in the rock, and the noise we made brought a woman out. 'Where do you live?' says I. 'Here, sir,' says she, and points to the hole in the rock. 'The children were all born here.' We went in. There was a large hollow cave. On one side was the chimney. Everything was clean and neat, though mean. There were shelves with earthenware and some pewter and brass. There was a whole side of bacon hanging up in the chimney. The woman said her husband worked in the lead mines. If he had good luck he could earn about fivepence a day. If she worked hard at washing the lead ore she could get threepence a day. So that was eightpence a day when they both worked hard, to maintain a man, his wife and five small children. Yet they seemed to live very pleasantly – the children looked plump and fat.

From Daniel Defoe, 'Tour through the Whole Island of Great Britain', 1726. This extract describes a cave near Wirksworth in Derbyshire. Defoe was a journalist and writer.

Hogarth

William Hogarth (1697–1764) taught himself to draw. When he was 14 years old he left school and trained as an engraver of silver tankards. Later he drew and engraved book illustrations. He was 30 years old before he learned to paint.

He had the idea of painting a set of pictures telling a story in the same was that a strip cartoon does today. From these he made engravings so that he could print copies. His pictures were full of life and action. They showed everyday scenes, mainly in London. Source C is the last of six pictures telling the life story of an idle apprentice. Before Hogarth's time most pictures in England were by foreign artists, showing rich people or religious subjects. Hogarth's prints sold well; he showed that an English artist could succeed. Others soon followed his example.

5.6 The First 'Prime Minister'

George I and George II used English nobles and gentry as **ministers** to run the country, just as other kings and queens had done. A group of the leading ministers were known as the **Cabinet**. This was because in earlier reigns they had met in the king's or queen's private room, or cabinet, at the palace.

But the first two Georges were foreigners who disliked London. They were happiest when they could go home to Hanover in Germany for a holiday. So it suited them to let the Cabinet work on its own.

The Cabinet had to get the king's agreement to everything the government did. So one of the ministers had to run the Cabinet meetings, and later go to court and get the king to agree to any decisions. He also had to get the MPs in the House of Commons to agree, because they voted the money to pay for everything.

Sir Robert Walpole was very successful at this job. He was leading minister for 21 years from 1721–42. Because he was the leader or 'first minister' he was sometimes called **Prime Minister** (from the French word *premier* meaning 'first'). This was only a nickname, not an official title; but later it became the usual name for the head of the govenment.

Most of the government offices were near the king's old palace of **Whitehall**. The Houses of Parliament were just round the corner. So Whitehall was a very convenient place for the Cabinet to meet. No. 10 Downing Street, just off Whitehall, has been the official home of the Prime Minister ever since Walpole.

Downing

Sir George Downing (1623?–84) was brought up in the American colonies, but came back to Britain to join Cromwell's army. He worked for Cromwell in Scotland, and became an MP and ambassador to the Netherlands. In 1660 he neatly changed sides and helped Charles II regain the throne. As a reward Charles knighted him and gave him land in London where Downing Street was later built. He held many important posts under Charles II, and died, rich and powerful, in 1684.

Robert Walpole was short and stout, weighing over 125kg. He was a country gentleman, like most other MPs, and spoke with a strong Norfolk accent. Although he became very rich, he still behaved like an ordinary country squire.

No. 10 Downing Street, rebuilt for Walpole in 1736. Dozens of houses looking just like this were built in London for merchants and gentry after the Great Fire of 1666.

6.1 The British Isles, 1500–1750

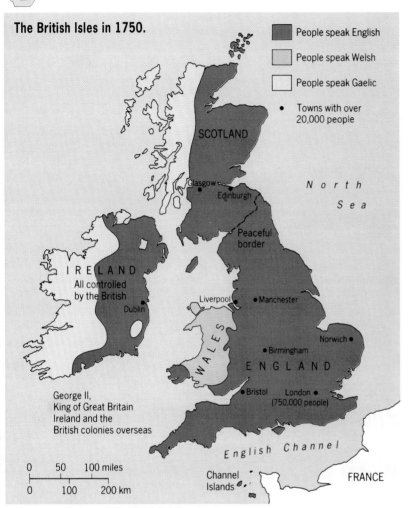

The British Isles in 1750.

Legend:
- People speak English
- People speak Welsh
- People speak Gaelic
- • Towns with over 20,000 people

SCOTLAND
Glasgow
Edinburgh
Peaceful border

IRELAND
All controlled by the British
Dublin

Liverpool • Manchester

WALES

Norwich •
• Birmingham

ENGLAND

• Bristol   London •
(750,000 people)

George II, King of Great Britain Ireland and the British colonies overseas

North Sea

English Channel

Channel Islands

FRANCE

0   50   100 miles
0   100   200 km

SCOTLAND
James IV, King of Scotland

English–Scots border: many battles and raids

North Sea

IRELAND
The Pale – fully controlled by the English
Dublin

York

WALES

Norwich

Oxford   London
Bristol   Canterbury
Exeter   Southampton

ENGLAND

Henry VII, King of England, Lord of Ireland, Prince of Wales

English Channel

Channel Islands   FRANCE

0   50   100 miles
0   100   200 km

The British Isles in 1500 (see page 4).

Changes

The changes of the years 1500–1750 were important. There were more people in Britain in 1750, not counting the people in the new Empire. It was during this time that the government in London took control of the British Isles. The new nation of Great Britain became richer because of trade and industry. Religion changed too – Britain broke from the Pope, and won a war against Catholic Spain. The English language spread. Britain took a lead in science. There were fine new buildings in London, and elegant country houses. From 1640–89 parliament forced the monarchs to let them help to run the country, and got rid of two kings who refused.

Can you pick a main change: that is one that caused many other changes, or matters most to us today, or mattered most to people at the time?

The population of the British Isles (and British settlers overseas), 1500 and 1750.

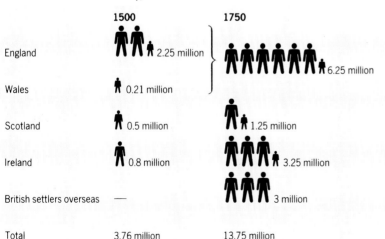

	1500	1750
England	2.25 million	6.25 million
Wales	0.21 million	
Scotland	0.5 million	1.25 million
Ireland	0.8 million	3.25 million
British settlers overseas	—	3 million
Total	3.76 million	13.75 million